JACKIE,
A
BOY,
AND A
DOG
A Warm Cold War Story

MARK D. BRUCE

Published by Clovercroft Publishing, Franklin, Tennessee.

JACKIE, A BOY, AND A DOG

A Warm Cold War Story

MARK D. BRUCE

DEDICATION

This book is dedicated to
my parents,
H. Byron and Doris Bruce;
my wife, Moira E. O'Brien-Bruce, DO;
our five children,
David, Daniel, Timothy,
Andrew, and Joanna;
and
Jacqueline Kennedy Onassis.

CONTENTS

ACKNOWLEDGEMENTS

There have been many people over the years that have encouraged me to write this story. Invariably when I tell my "dog story," be it at a private dinner party, or to a larger audience at a civic club or church group, there are those that approach me afterward to ask if I have written a book yet. And although my own children have had a vague awareness of the "dog story," I found them unaware of the lessons to be found therein.

When I was approached by Blur Films, Madrid, Spain, to do a documentary for Audi Automobiles, about the Legacy of Strelka (Streaker's grandmother), I finally realized the deeper importance of what *Jackie, A Boy, and a Dog* could be. I wanted to preserve these events as part of my legacy for my children and grandchildren, and to have them — and all who read this book — understand how God intervenes in our lives and prepares us for His service.

Without the support of Moira, my wife, and much input from my mom, Doris Bruce, my brothers, Ron and David, this work would not have been completed.

Many thanks to Sharla Fritz, who came along at a critical juncture to provide significant writing and editing guidance, setting aside her own projects to help me.

Without the encouragement of Tammy Kling, Debbie Sheppard, and Patti Lusk, of OnFire Books Leadership Company, this book would still be years from completion.

A special thank you to my brother-in-law, Jim O'Brien, for introducing me to Tammy Kling.

My pastors, Stuart Briscoe and Julius R. Malone, have been so important in my spiritual growth and development, and provided insights into the text.

Larry Carpenter, CEO of Clovercroft Publishing, has given invaluable guidance through the labyrinth of the publishing world. Thanks Larry.

And most important, thanks be to God, my Lord and Savior, for His divine intervention in my life. To God be the glory.

JACKIE,
A
BOY,
AND A
PUP
A Warm Cold War Story

How a 10-year-old son of a Baptist preacher, made friends with the President's wife, and got a dog.

CHAPTER ONE:
THE SUMMER OF 1963

I squinted in the sunshine, the weight of smooth wood in my hands. Squinting back at me from his mound, the pitcher stood ready to hurl the next ball. Under an azure-blue sky, playing with my friends in my backyard, how could summer vacation get any better than this? I adjusted my feet in an attempt to match the stance of my baseball hero, Stan "The Man" Musial. Hunching over the plate just a bit, I waited for the slow, pudgy duck of a pitch to arc toward me. As it approached—belt high, right in my wheelhouse—I was determined not to whiff. My Louisville slugger shot forward, slicing the air with all the force my ten-year-old arms could muster.

Little did I know that one swing would lead to a heartbreaking tragedy, a connection with a First Lady, and an understanding that our God in heaven has control, even in the midst of chaos.

A PLACE OF SAFETY

It was the summer of 1963. Trouble in the world filled news reports on the television and the cloud of the Cold War[1] hung over our heads. The Bay of Pigs incident in the spring of 1961 had tarnished America's blue-chip image. The existential threat of the Cuban Missile Crisis in October 1962 had frightened the nation. Civil unrest had grown with riots in Birmingham, Alabama, that May. Martin Luther King Jr., had emerged as a respected leader, one who would continue to have an impact on the whole nation and even the world, well into the future.

I had an awareness of all of this. I sensed a lingering fear that catastrophe on an unimaginable scale lurked just around the corner, ready to envelop us. Even as a young boy, I perceived a certain sense of foreboding, feeling it in the adults around me—my parents, my teachers at school, and all those I looked up to. Hope for the future had dimmed.

At least, it had for much of the nation. While I was aware of these things, the everyday held far too many distractions and pleasures to allow me too much trepidation. In fact, for a ten-year-old boy growing up in Middle America, life was sublime. As a part of a whole generation of baby boomers,

---

1   See appendix 1.

growing up amidst a life of post World War II prosperity, I didn't spend a lot of time dwelling on the mayhem. I believed in a bright future.

The college town of Columbia, Missouri, served as a perfect backdrop to an idyllic childhood. In my quiet suburban neighborhood, I could ride my bike to my friend's house, explore Bear Creek with its frogs and crawdads, and play baseball with my friends. We felt safe and secure— what was crime?

My brothers and I attended Parkade Elementary School, only five blocks away from our home. Dad was a Baptist minister, and both of my parents earned the respect of the community. As pastor's kids, my brothers and I had the run of Memorial Baptist. I can still picture the redbrick church with white pillars that we attended every Wednesday night and twice on Sundays. Though the world outside may have been fraught with danger and uncertainty, safety and security seemed to wrap around our town like a blanket. It seemed a peace that nothing could disturb.

A HERO AT HOME PLATE

Of all the distractions available to me, I especially loved baseball—in particular, the St. Louis Cardinals. That summer of 1963 proved to be the last in the illustrious career of Stan "The Man" Musial, the star player for the Cardinals. At forty-two, he still hit an average of .251 and closed out his 22-year career with a lifetime batting average of .331, having set National League records in career hits (3,630), runs batted in (1,951), games played (3,026), at bats (10,972), runs scored (1,949), and doubles (725). A seven-time batting champion, Musial was named the National League's MVP three times and led the Cardinals to three World Series Championships.

As a kid, I didn't memorize statistics. But my head was filled with the fantasy of being Stan the Man every time I went up to bat. Like him, I "swung for the fences." Musial's baseball career was ending as my life was just beginning. Unbeknownst to him, he would impact me in a most profound way on that summer day.

Baseball consumed summer life on our street. My family had the biggest yard on the block, so it became the neighborhood gathering place for baseball games. Because our backyard backed up against a major highway, a six-foot chain-link fence stood where our lot ended. It took a solid hit to clear that fence, so any hit that made it that far became an automatic home run. The highway was located on an elevated embankment, so we never hit any vehicles.

When the weather warmed, almost every day included a baseball game. My brothers and I had chores to do, but after we finished them, it was game on. A few neighborhood kids always joined up with the three Bruce boys for exciting baseball play. We had no real home plate, just a worn spot on the field. No one pitched to strike the batter out. That would just waste time as choosy batters would wait for their pitch. Balls and strikes didn't much matter. Bunts? No way. Everyone wanted to hit—and hit as hard as they could.

A FRIEND AT PLAY

Even more than baseball, I loved dogs. I came out of the womb of a dog lover. I think my first sentence was, "Can I have a dog?" I can't explain this natural canine affinity, other than to say that God made me that way. Dog lovers know what I mean. Our family had other pets, mostly cats, but they never seemed to capture my heart the way dogs did.

As parents of active boys, my mom and dad constantly looked for wholesome activities for their children. So when the 4-H program started up in the part of Columbia where we lived, I think they thought it might help me stay out of trouble. 4-H offered a lot of ways to get involved, and I was especially excited about the dog care program that taught kids grooming, feeding, obedience training, and general responsibility for a dog. I figured that if I got into the 4-H Dog Care Program, I would have to get a dog—and it worked! So, at age nine, I acquired a mutt named Midget. Through a 4-H leader's network, I received Midget free of charge (very important to us, since we didn't have a lot of money). This energetic, super-fast canine fulfilled my dog longings and became my loyal companion.

Baseball and Midget filled that summer of 1963. She loved to play ball as much as I did. I hardly had to teach her to fetch, and she could play catch with a baseball with remarkable finesse. If it was Mom and Dad's intent to keep me out of trouble, it worked. We spent hours after school playing.

A TRAGEDY AT BAT

On that fateful day, I found myself at bat, with a fantasy of Stan the Man whirling in my head. Fantasy has been the failing of many a man, and this time it would cost me greatly. I can still smell the scent of freshly cut grass and feel the humidity of that hot June day in central Missouri. It was perfect baseball weather. When my turn at bat arrived, I stood at the "plate," rubbed some dirt on my hands, dug in my PF Flyers, and choked up on the bat just enough to copy my hero. Stan the Man would be retiring soon, so he would be swinging for the fences even more than usual… and so would I. When I saw the pitch, I knew it would get me a home run. I swung with all my might.

But, instead of the satisfying crack of my bat against the ball, I heard a sickening thud. I had assumed Midget was in the house. She wasn't. My best canine friend and expert ball catcher had been standing dutifully behind me. When she saw the baseball approaching home plate, she thought it was meant for her. With a horror of synchrony, she leapt to catch the ball just as I made my perfect "Stan the Man" cut.

1963: Ten-year old Mark Bruce is involved in a
4H dog-care project with his puppy Midget.
Mark was playing baseball one day.
It was his turn at bat . . .

In so many aspects of life, timing is everything. How I wish my timing had been off that day. If only I had been more like Mighty Casey at bat instead of Stan the Man. I hit Midget squarely in the head, and she died instantly, not making a sound. I screamed in anguish. Hot tears mixed with sweat and humidity as I stood over her lifeless body, flooded with both grief and disbelief at what had just happened. I had destroyed the very one I loved.

I continued to cry for a week, constantly wracked with guilt and loneliness. Inconsolable, I came out of the bedroom I shared with my brother only to eat and use the restroom. The instant replay of my swinging bat and leaping dog went through my mind again and again. I couldn't think of anything but Midget and that surreal moment. The marathon of grief warped time. What had happened in a second took an eternity to endure.

Had the incident happened today, I would have been in counseling, but those resources were unheard of then. Although my parents attempted to comfort me and my friends tried to console me, nothing quenched my sorrow. My love for Midget hurt. My love for baseball stung as aftershocks of bitter grief and remorse ebbed and flowed.

Even if I had not been fully aware of the mayhem of the world in the 1960s, I now faced my own personal tragedy.

Life is bigger than ourselves, for we live in a world where there is a God, and He often intervenes in the most unexpected of ways. But on that day, He didn't seem to intervene, leaving me heartbroken and in despair. Later, I learned that He knew my pain and would choose His time to act. He opened my eyes to the world around me, a world far bigger than my life in Columbia, Missouri.

John F. Kennedy is elected 35th President of the United States

January 20, 1961

Soviet Premier Nikita Khrushchev demonstrating the durability of Russian shoes to the UN while defending his country's dominant influence in Eastern Europe on October 12, 1960.

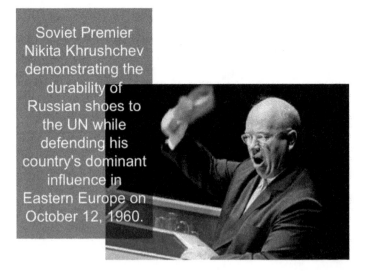

Chapter Two:
PUPNIKS

And now for the rest of the story...

The expansion of my world began with Paul Harvey's radio broadcast, which my parents faithfully listened to in those days. One summer day not long after the death of Midget, the legendary newsman and commentator would announce something that would change my life and connect me with the First Lady of the United States. To understand the context for that announcement, however, we must go to Vienna.

A SUMMIT AND A SPACE PUP

The story begins with the 1961 Vienna Summit Conference[2], where the leaders of the world's two superpowers in the Cold War era met. President John F. Kennedy of the United

---

2   See appendix 2.

States and Premier Nikita Khrushchev of the Soviet Union sat down together to discuss issues between their two countries. Contact between the two heads of state began with a letter Khrushchev sent to Kennedy on November 9, 1960, congratulating the new president on his victory. In the letter, Khrushchev also expressed a desire to negotiate with the United States on the issues of disarmament and the easing of international tensions. Kennedy and Khrushchev continued to correspond, and on February 22, 1961, Kennedy sent Khrushchev a letter stating, "I hope it will be possible, before too long, for us to meet personally for an informal exchange of views."[3] The president thought that if he could get the Soviet leader to come to the table, they could work out their conflicts. Other American diplomats advised Kennedy not to meet with Khrushchev, fearing the young president had misjudged his rival's intentions.

However, the two leaders continued their plans, and in June of 1961, they met in Vienna. There they discussed topics related to Berlin, Laos, and the Bay of Pigs in Cuba. At first, the meeting was seen as a diplomatic triumph, but in retrospect, President Kennedy had a very inauspicious foreign policy debut at this summit. It was overly ambitious and naïve for the young president to attempt to charm the Russians into Cold War submission and give up their aspirations of world domination.

---

3   Wikipedia contributors, "Vienna Summit," Wikipedia, The Free Encyclopedia, https://en.wikipedia.org/wiki/Vienna_summit.

Jaqueline Kennedy received a "Space puppy" from Khrushev

At a dinner during the summit between US president. John F. Kennedy and Soviet leader Nikita Khrushchev in Vienna in June 1961, Khrushchev sat next to the president's wife Jaqueline Kennedy. He bragged about the flight of Soviet space dogs and told Mrs. Kennedy about the puppies of the space dog Strelka. Out of lack of dinner topics and more as a joke, she said to Khrushchev, "couldn't you send me one?" She did not think more about it until two months later when Soviet ambassador Menshikov, during a visit to the White House, delivered one of the puppies to an astonounded Mrs. Kennedy.

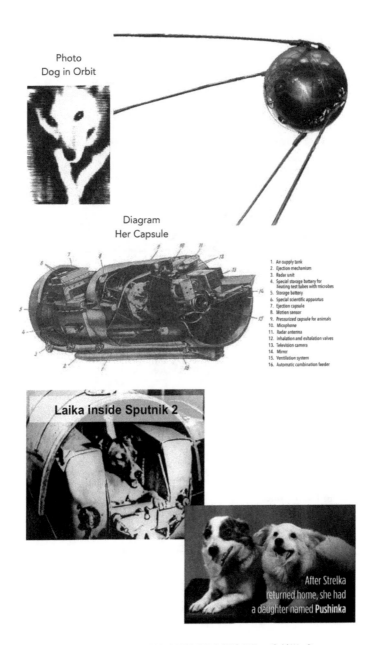

Photo
Dog in Orbit

Diagram
Her Capsule

1. Air-supply tank
2. Ejection mechanism
3. Radar unit
4. Special storage battery for heating test tubes with microbes
5. Storage battery
6. Special scientific apparatus
7. Ejection capsule
8. Motion sensor
9. Pressurized capsule for animals
10. Microphone
11. Radar antenna
12. Inhalation and exhalation valves
13. Television camera
14. Mirror
15. Ventilation system
16. Automatic combination feeder

Laika inside Sputnik 2

After Strelka returned home, she had a daughter named **Pushinka**

Russian dogs STRELKA and BELKA went into space aboard Sputnik 5 and returned healthy (NASA Archives)

They are preserved at Memorial Museum of Astronautics. Belka and Strelka Korabl-Sputnik-2 (Spaceship Satellite-2), also known as Sputnik 5, was launced on August 19, 1960. On board were the dogs Belka (Squirrel) and Strelka (Little Arrow). Also on board were 40 mice, 2 rats, and a variety of plants.

After a day in orbit, the spacecraft's retrorocket was fired and the landing capsule and the dogs were safely recovered. They were the first living animals to survive orbital flight.

Strelka later gave birth to six puppies, one of which was given to Caroline Kennedy, daughter of US President John F. Kennedy, but Soviet premier Nikita Khrushchev.

Today, the bodies of Strelka and Belka remain preserved at the Memorial Museum of Astronautics in Moscow. Belka sits in a glass case in the museum while Strelka is part of a traveling exhibit that has visited the US, China, Australia, Israel, and other countries.

June 21, 1961

Dear Mr. Chairman:

I want to express to you my very great appreciation for your thoughtfulness in sending to me the model of an American whaler, which we discussed while in Vienna. It now rests in my office here in the White House.

Mrs. Kennedy and I were particularly pleased to receive 'Pushinka'. Her flight from the Soviet Union to the United States was not as dramatic as the flight of her mother, nevertheless, it was a long voyage and she stood it well. We both appreciate your remembering these matters in your busy life.

We send to you, your wife and your family our very best wishes.

Sincerely yours,

His Excellency
Nikita S. Khrushchev
Chairman of the Council of Ministers of the
Union of Soviet Socialist Republics
Moscow

Even though the president could not claim diplomatic victory, First Lady Jacqueline Kennedy had some success at the state dinner by enchanting Premier Khrushchev. The Summit Conference took place in the context of the early Space Race.[4] The Soviets had experienced recent success with the live return of two dogs sent into space aboard the *Sputnik* spacecraft, becoming known to the world as Strelka and Belka, and referred to as space dogs.[5] These dogs were strays, "volunteering" for the Soviet Space Program and so becoming heroes of the Soviet Empire. After their return, Strelka had a litter of pups, which gained international attention. At the Summit Conference State Dinner, Strelka's "space pups" became a topic of the evening. First Lady Kennedy, while making small talk with the Soviet Premier, not very seriously suggested that he should give her one of the pups. Everyone had a good chuckle about this, but since animals had become the Kennedys' preferred gift of state, the Soviets took the comment more seriously than Mrs. Kennedy had intended.

In a letter to the White House shortly following the Vienna Summit, Premier Khrushchev wrote of the gifts he was sending the American First Family—a model of a nineteenth-century sail-steam vessel carved from a walrus tusk (President Kennedy having remarked on his love of collecting ship models) and another present, meant for the First Lady. "It is also a pleasure," the Soviet Premiere wrote, "for Nina Petrovna and myself to fulfill Mrs. Kennedy's wish and to send to you and

---

4   See appendix 3.
5   See appendix 4.

your family little 'Pushinka,' a direct offspring of the well known cosmos-traveler 'Strelka,' which made a trip in a cosmic ship on August 19, 1960, and successfully returned to earth."[6]

A few weeks later, the Soviet Ambassador arrived at the White House with a fluffy white puppy to give to the First Family, who, of course, graciously accepted the pup into their household. In his reply letter, dated June 21, 1961, Kennedy wrote to Khrushchev of his gratitude for the gifts of both the model and the puppy, remarking, "Mrs. Kennedy and I were particularly pleased to receive 'Pushinka.' Her flight from the Soviet Union to the United States was not as dramatic as the flight of her mother, nevertheless, it was a long voyage and she stood it well."[7]

A LITTER IN THE WHITE HOUSE

Kennedy's poor performance in Vienna haunted his administration and, some have alleged, caused the Soviets to underestimate the resolve and competence of the young president, resulting in an overreach in the Soviet foreign policy objectives and actions. This led to the Cuban Missile Crisis in October of 1962.

---

6   Kenneth P. O'Donnell and David F. Powers with Joe McCarthy, *"Johnny, We Hardly Knew Ye": Memories of John Fitzgerald Kennedy* (Boston and Toronto: Little, Brown and Company, 1972,1973), 347–348.

7   Office of the Historian, Bureau of Public Affairs, US Department of State, "17. Letter From President Kennedy to Chairman Khrushchev," https:// history.state.gov/historicaldocuments/frus1961-63v06/d17.

The dogs of President Kennedy

From his early years through his political career, John Kennedy was an avid dog lover. He was usually photographed with retrievers or setters. During the White House years, he requested that the dogs be trained to greet the Presidential helicopter when it arrived back at the White House. The Presidential dogs included an Irish wolfhound, a German shepherd, and an Irish cocker spaniel.

Caroline and son John Jr. join President Kennedy at the White House

Presidential dog Charlie gets attention from Caroline Kennedy as the president, his son, John, and Mrs. Kennedy look on with Pushinka's puppies Blackie and White Tips and family dogs Shannon, Clipper, and Wolfie. (Courtesy of John Fitzgerald Kennedy Presidential Library and Museum)

The Kennedys come with a menagerie of pets, including their Welsh terrier, Charlie

IN HAPPIER DAYS, Caroline Kennedy raced after her Welsh terrier, Charlie, who had scooted away as the family deplaned at Andrews Air Force Base after vacation.

PET. A three-year-old black and white springer spaniel, Champion Wakefield's Black Knight, owned by Mrs. W. J. S. Boric of Gwynedd Valley, Pa., won best-in-show at the 87th annual Westminster Kennel

Kennedy sent Butterfly, a female, to 10 year Karen House of Westchester, Ill., a Chicago sub Straker, a male, was given to Mark Bruce, of of Columbia, Mo.

Pushinka, a dog gifted by Nikita Khrushchev,
Premier of the Soviet Union

As a sign of friendship and a peace offering, Soviet Premier Khrushchev gave Caroline Kennedy a furry mongrel named Pushinka, who was the puppy of a Russian space dog Strelka. Not worrying about differing ideologies, Pushinka and Charlie had four puppies together. The President referred to them as the pupniks.

Charlie and Pushinka on the White House lawn

Cuban Missile Crisis
October 14 – 28, 1962

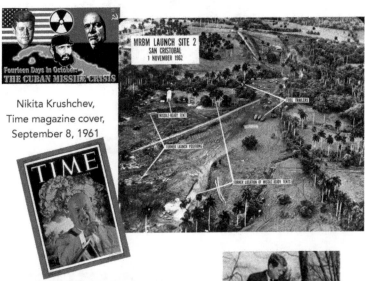

Nikita Krushchev,
Time magazine cover,
September 8, 1961

At the height of the Cuban missle crisis when there was some doubt about whether civilzation as we knew it would last beyond the next day or explode in a nuclear holocaust, President Kennedy had Charlie (a little Welsh terrier who was his daughter Caroline's dog) brought to the chaos of the War room.

Traphes Bryant, the White house kennel keeper, describes the events.

"I was there in Jack Kennedy's office that day. Everything was in an uproar. I was then feet from Kennedy's desk as Pierre Salinger ran around the office taking messages and issuing orders while the President sat looking awfully worried. There was talk about the Russian fleet coming in and our fleet blocking them off. It looked like war. Our of thte blue, Kennedy suddenly called for Charlie to be brought to his office."

After petting Charlie for a while, the president relaxed, gave Charlie back to the kennel keeper, and calmly said, "I suppose that it's time to make some decisions."

The President made some decisions. The Russians backed off. The world went on.

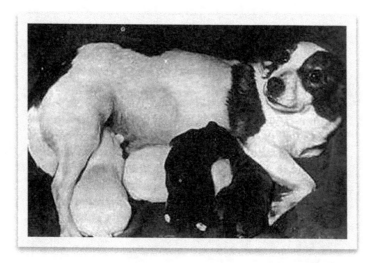

Strelka with her puppies .

In the midst of the chaos and confusion of the missile crisis, President Kennedy found comfort in the company of Charlie, the family's Welsh terrier, having the kennel handler bring Charlie to the White House War Room. After about ten minutes of playing with Charlie, President Kennedy was able to refocus on the crisis, helping him to make key decisions that profoundly influenced the survival of Western civilization.

Eight months later, Charlie sired a litter of four pups by Pushinka. President Kennedy nicknamed the litter the "pupniks" (a play on the name of the *Sputnik* spacecraft), and when they were born on June 15, 1963, the whole nation delighted in these famous dogs. Suddenly, the White House kennels were bursting.

This plethora of First Dogs led to the statement by Paul Harvey that changed my life.

A PUPNIK
BIRTH ANNOUNCEMENT

One day that June, my mother, brothers, and I were listening to our plastic tabletop radio with a radial dial as we ate lunch at the kitchen table. We faithfully listened to "Paul Harvey News and Commentary" every day, but that day the broadcast seized my attention. The venerated newsman told the story of Pushinka's offspring and the sudden excess of puppies at the White House. Harvey wondered aloud, "What are they going to do with all those dogs?" My ears immediately perked up. And I thought I might have an answer, at least regarding one of the pupniks.

The loss of Midget had created a huge void in my life. But perhaps the abundance of dogs at the White House could be an answer to prayer. I needed a new canine companion and a pet for my 4-H dog care project. Why not one of the dogs Paul Harvey talked about? Consequently, I announced to my family that I would write the First Family and ask for one of the puppies.

My two older brothers thought my plan was amusing, to say the least, especially in light of Midget's recent demise. I could feel their skeptical stares and see the rolling of their eyes, not to mention hearing their not-too-subtle snide remarks. But I was undaunted. Eventually I discovered that God's intervention in our lives, so clear and evident to us, may not be understood by others. God reaches out to the small and humble. Even my Baptist minister father, although a godly man thoroughly versed in Scripture, could not suspend his disbelief when faced with the reality of divine intervention within his own household.

I couldn't conceive that the First Lady, or President Kennedy, could find a more deserving home for one of the pups. With Mom's approval, I set about writing Mrs. Kennedy, explaining my situation, and asking for one of the pupniks.[8] I pled my case as well as a ten-year-old could, then put the letter in the mail, hoping it was good enough.

I wrote bluntly and to the point. My letter essentially said, "I killed my dog. May I have one of yours?" I didn't use my very real emotional trauma to play on her heart—I was a guileless young boy. Manipulating myself into the heart of the First Lady was not my intent.

---

8   Of all the letters I was to write to Jacqueline Kennedy, including this one to the White House, this is the only one for which I have the word-for-word contents, because it was preserved. I never photocopied or made duplicates of all the others, so I can only remember the general contents of what I wrote. On the other hand, I kept all the letters from Mrs. Kennedy, and these are presented in original form in this book.

Dear Mrs. Kennedy,

The other day I heard on the radio that the dog Mr. Kruschev gave to you had pups and you didn't know what to do with them. On June the 8th I was playing baseball. I was batting. Our dog Midget go behind me when I was swinging the bat and I accidentally hit her in the head. She died almost immeditly. I am a member of the Parkade 4 H. Midget was my project. I was in dog care. If you would let me have one of the pups I could continue in 4 H.

The transportation may be a problem. My dad and brother and a few other boys will be going to Washington, D.C. for National R.A. Congress. If you will let us have it they could pick it up.

Thank you very much for your cooperation.

       Your friend,

         Mark Bruce

During the next week I eagerly checked the mail daily, and, sure enough, a letter arrived from the White House. Nancy Tuckerman, Jacqueline Kennedy's personal secretary and confidant, explained that the White House would not distribute the dogs. Specifically, it stated:

---

9   Royal Ambassadors (RA) is a Christian boys' Scout-like organization run by the Woman's Missionary Union of the Southern Baptist Convention (SBC). About three thousand SBC churches sponsor groups.

THE WHITE HOUSE
WASHINGTON

June 22, 1963

Dear Mark,

I am writing on behalf of Mrs. Kennedy to
thank you for your letter of June 19.

We were very sorry to read of the accident
to your dog, Midget; however, we regret that
there are no puppies available for distribution
from The White House. We appreciate the
interest which prompted you to write.

With all best wishes,

Sincerely,

Nancy Tuckerman

Nancy Tuckerman
Social Secretary

Master Mark Bruce
106 Texas Avenue
Columbia, Missouri

THE WHITE HOUSE

Master Mark Bruce
106 Texas Avenue
Columbia, Missouri

I was devastated. I felt deflated. The guilt of my lethal act returned, as did self-doubt. I couldn't see any hope on the horizon. Maybe my brothers were right in their snide remarks.

Yet, the story wasn't over. God continued to work on my behalf. Looking back, I realize God hears the cry of our hearts. He may seem slow to act. It may appear that He doesn't care. But the events in our lives may become intense classrooms of faith. Hebrews 11:1 tells us *"faith is the assurance of things hoped for, the conviction of things not seen"* (NASB). This kind of faith must walk hand in hand with patience, because God has His own timing, and sometimes He doesn't exactly meet our schedule.

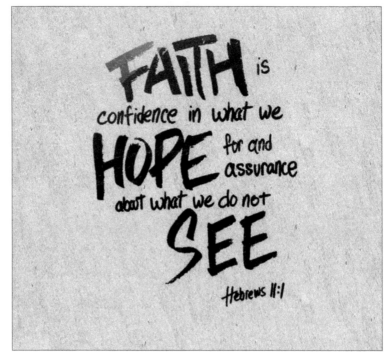

COLUMBIA DAILY TRIBUNE

COLUMBIA, MO., MONDAY, AUGUST 19, 1963 *Page one* PRICE 10c   FOU

Streaker, a White House Pup, to Arrive Here Tomorrow as Gift to Mark Bruce

These two White House puppies, Streaker, a male, left, and Butterfly, a female, are on their way today to Mark Bruce, 9, of Columbia, and Karen House, 10, of Westchester, Ill. Streaker is scheduled to arrive here by air freight on an Ozark Air Lines flight scheduled to land at the Municipal Airport at 7:53 a. m. tomorrow. Streaker will leave Washington at five minutes before midnight tonight, Columbia time, on an Eastern Air Lines flight to St. Louis, arriving there at 3:39 a.m. He will be placed on the Ozark flight at 6:45 a.m. (CST). (Wirephoto)

Speechless when he first heard yesterday morning that the White House was sending him one of the puppies, Mark Bruce soon displayed a wide grin reflecting his happiness in receiving a replacement for his former pet, Midget. (Tribune photo)

KP18X
COLUMBIA, MO., AUG. 19 (UPI)--THE SON OF A MINISTER HERE
WILL BE GETTING A NEW DOG SOON--FROM THE PRESIDENT AND MRS. KENNEDY.
MARK BRUCE, 10, SON OF THE REV. AND MRS. BYRON BRUCE, WAS
NOTIFIED YESTERDAY THAT THE PRESIDENTIAL FAMILY HAD SELECTED HIM
TO RECEIVE "STREAKER" FROM THE LITTER OF "PUSINKA," AN OFFSPRING OF
THE RUSSIAN SPACE DOG "STRELKA."
     "I GUESS I WAS PICKED BECAUSE MY DOG GOT KILLED," MARK SAID.
THE YOUTH WROTE THE PRESIDENT IN JUNE TELLING HIM THAT HIS DOG
".CS&39" HAD BEEN KILLED AND HE NEEDED ANOTHER ANIMAL TO CONTINUE
HIS 4-H DOG CARE PROJECT.
     MARK'S EARLIER DOG WAS KILLED WHEN ACCIDENTALLY STRUCK BY A
BASEBALL BAT.
     "ALL THE BOYS AT SUNDAY SCHOOL WERE KIND OF ENVIOUS OF HIM,"
REV. BRUCE SAID YESTERDAY. "I THOUGHT HE WAS FOOLING AT FIRST WHEN
HE TOLD ME THE GOOD NEWS."
                    TG&8ACG

Chapter Three:
SURPRISE

As it turned out, God's schedule included some surprises. Our gracious heavenly Father reassures us that He *"is able to do immeasurably more than all we ask or imagine, according to his power that is at work within us"* (Ephesians 3:20). Yet we often forget this. At ten I certainly didn't understand all that meant, but I would soon find out.

First, though, I had to deal with my disappointment. Yes, I had some small satisfaction that someone had heard my sad story and acknowledged it, but the frustration that I didn't have a dog persisted. So I began to implement plan B: Get a dog from the Humane Society. Almost every day for the next two months, I asked Mom if we could go to the dog pound (as we called it in 1963) and get a dog. I was nothing if not persistent, and it probably drove my mother nuts.

BACK AT THE WHITE HOUSE

Even as I kept "dogging" Mom with my requests, God continued to work behind the scenes on my behalf at the White House. I thought I was the only child who asked the First Lady for one of Pushinka's puppies. But it turns out thousands of other children sent letters and wrote essays. Much later in life, I learned the surprising backstory of the distribution of the pupniks.

The First Lady approached Traphes Bryant, the kennel keeper at the White House, with an idea for finding good homes for the puppies of the Russian dog. The president had arranged for Bryant to bring the dogs to Hyannis Port, Massachusetts, where the Kennedy family vacationed for the summer. But eventually Jacqueline realized her family simply had too many dogs. She thought an essay contest would solve that problem and perhaps generate positive publicity for the White House. Caroline, her daughter, agreed with the plan, happy that children who had no dogs would now receive pets. She had named the dogs, but gave the recipients permission to change the names of the dogs if they wanted.[10]

President and Mrs. Kennedy had already received letters from children around the country about the dogs. One letter had particularly amused the president—because of its spelling and content:

---

10   Helen Thomas, "Two Puppy Dreams Come True," *The Washington Post*, August 19, 1963.

Dear Mr. President,

Please don't throw this leter away until you read it.

When you were runing for President my sister and I held banners that said "VOTE FOR KENNEDY" and we sang a song, "Kennedy in the White House, Nixon in the garbage can."

You are doing a good job and we love you.

I read in the newspaper that Carylon's dog had puppies. My sister has been dying for a puppie. Do you think Carylon will mind very much if she gave us a puppie? It will have a good home. Do you know what it means to get a puppie from the President of the United States?

All the best,
Tom

[11]

Letters like this inspired Mrs. Kennedy to offer an essay contest that would not only shine a positive light on the White House but also provide a way to find good homes for two of Pushinka's pups. However, she had concerns about this plan.

---

11 Traphes Bryant with Frances Spatz Leighton, *Dog Days at the White House: The Outrageous Memoirs of the Presidential Kennel Keeper* (New York: Macmillan Publishing Co., 1975), 60.

She asked Bryant if he thought a child would take good care of the dog. The kennel keeper reassured her that most children treat their dogs well—maybe even better than their parents. He also pointed out that whoever won the contest would have the eyes of their whole community on them. The new owners wouldn't dare mistreat the Pushinka pups.[12]

With that reassurance, Mrs. Kennedy implemented the contest. And as an added measure to make sure the dog would be treated well, she stipulated that the children write about how they would care for the new pet.

The White House received an avalanche of replies. Bryant writes that he didn't save the letters but vividly remembered an unsigned funny one that promised the kid would "raise the dog to be a Democrat and bite Republicans."[13] He didn't trust the source of that letter—thinking that someone working at the White House had probably written it. Perhaps Pierre Salinger?

My letter turned out to be one of

thousands. How could it possibly hope

to catch the eye of the First Lady?

---

12   Bryant, *Dog Days*, 59–60.
13   Bryant, *Dog Days*, 60.

Mark's Letter

"Dear Mrs. Kennedy:

"The other day I heard on the radio that the dog Mr. Kruschev (sic) gave to you had pups and you didn't know what to do with them. On June the 8th I was playing baseball. I was batting. Our dog Midget got behind me when I was swinging the bat and I accidentally hit her in the head. She died almost immeditly (sic). I am a member of the Parkade 4 H. Midget was my project. I was in dog care. If you would let me have one of the pups I could continue in 4 H.

"The transportation may be a problem. My dad and brothers and few other boys will be going to Washington, D. C., for National R. A. Congress. If you will let us have it they could pick it up.

"Thank you very much for your cooperation. Your friend,   "Mark Bruce."

United Press International

STREAKER IS HIS: Mark Bruce of Columbia, Mo., has an empty dog bed, idle leash, and unused rubber bone (lately) all ready for the puppy he'll get today. The youngest of three brothers, Mark lost his dog in a baseball accident. His mother, Mrs. H. Myron Bruce, received the call from the President's secretary. His father is a minister.

Karen's Letter

Karen's letter to the President, written in late July in pencil on tablet paper:

"Dear Mr. President:

"I would like to have one of your pretty dog puppies. I would like a puppy so much because I never had a dog before and I like your dog verry (sic) much. If you give me a puppy I will be so happy.

"P. S. Write me back and answer my letter please Mr. Kennedy. I don't know how to spell the name of the dog that just had the babbies (sic).

"Sincerely yours,

"Karen House."

Associated Press

BUTTERFLY IS HERS: Until yesterday Karen House of Westchester, Ill., had only guppies for pets. Now she'll have a new female puppy to care for and Caroline Kennedy says she can even change its name. Her father, Harold House, an air conditioning salesman, answered the call from the White House.

Newark, N. J., Monday, August 19, 1963

Caroline 'OKs' gifts of puppies

Jerry Pappalardo
463 SO. 16 TH ST.
NEWARK, NEW JERSEY

Butterfly (right) and Streaker (left) will go to two lucky children

(AP WIREPHOTO)

HYANNIS PORT, Mass. (UPI)—An Illinois girl and a boy from Columbia, Mo., in a deal "cleared" by Caroline Kennedy, today received Presidential gifts—two of the latest additions to the White House kennel.

Karen House, 10, of the Chicago suburb of Westchester, and Mark Bruce, 9, whose father is a minister, were picked by President and Mrs. Kennedy from among 5,000 letter-writing children who asked for the dogs.

They were born June 14 to Pushinka, a mongrel, and five-year-old Caroline's Welsh terrier, Charlie. Pushinka is the offspring of the famous Russian space dog Strelka. She was sent as a gift to Mrs. Kennedy in June, 1961, by Soviet Premier Nikita S. Khrushchev.

Karen will get "Butterfly," a female, and Mark will receive "Streaker," a male.

The dogs were named by Caroline, who "cleared" the gift, Press Secretary Pierre Salinger told newsmen. He said the girl was "very enthusiastic" about giving the puppies to children who did not have dogs.

"The puppy will be taken care of so well it won't be funny," Karen said yesterday when she learned of the gift. "We have a big yard. Caro-

Karen House and her parents
(AP WIREPHOTO)

line already has named the dog 'Butterfly' so I'm going to keep that name.

"I guess I got picked because my dog got killed," Mark said at home.

"I thought he was fooling at first," Rev. Bruce said. "All the boys at Sunday school were kind of envious of him this morning."

The puppies will ride to Washington today aboard Kennedy's jetliner. Then they will be shipped to Karen and Mark, at Kennedy's expense.

Letters poured into the White House, mostly from children, after the puppies were born on Flag Day.

The First Lady heard of the letters from youngsters all over the country requesting one of the puppies while she was in the hospital after the birth of Patrick Bouvier Kennedy, who died two days later.

She asked the White House correspondence section to pick 10 representative letters and send them to her. From the letters she selected the two children to be given the puppies.

Mark's appeal was based on the fact that his dog "Midget" had died "when I was swinging the bat and I accidentally hit her in the head." He told Mrs. Kennedy that Midget was his "Dog Care" project in the 4-H and if he had one of

(Please turn to Page 2, Col. 3)

Mark and mom prepare bed for Streaker
(UPI TELEPHOTO)

New York Herald Tribune   M. 19, 1963

CAROLINE SENDS THEM GIFTS

"I never had a dog before and I like your dog verry much."

Associated Press wirephoto

THANK-YOU SMILE—Karen House, 10, of Chicago, sits with her father Harold and beams gratitude for the gift to her of "Butterfly," Pushinka's pup.

Herald Tribune—UPI telephoto

BOY'S WELCOME—Mark Bruce, 10, and his mother, Mrs. Byron Bruce, glow in anticipation of the arrival in Columbia, Mo., of Streaker, another Pushinka offspring.

By United Press International

HYANNIS PORT, Mass.

An Illinois girl and a boy from Columbia, Mo., in a deal "cleared" by Caroline Kennedy, yesterday received Presidential gifts—two of the latest additions to the White House kennel.

Karen House, 10, of the Chicago suburb of Westchester, and Mark Bruce, 9, whose father is a minister, were picked by President and Mrs. Kennedy from among 5,000 letter-writing children who asked for the dogs.

They were born June 14 to Pushinka, a mongrel, and Caroline's Welsh terrier, Charlie. Pushinka is the offspring of the famous Russian space dog Strelka. She was sent as a gift to Mrs. Kennedy in June, 1961, by Soviet Premier Nikita S. Khrushchev.

Karen will get Butterfly, a female, and Mark will receive Streaker, a male.

The dogs were named by Caroline, 5½, who "cleared" the gift, press secretary Pierre Salinger told newsmen. He said the girl was "very enthusiastic" about giving the puppies to children who did not have dogs.

"The puppy will be taken care of so well it won't be funny," Karen said yesterday when she learned of the gift. "We have a big yard. Caroline already has named the dog Butterfly so I'm going to keep that name.

The puppies will ride to Washington today aboard Mr. Kennedy's jetliner. Then they will be shipped to Karen and Mark, at Mr. Kennedy's expense.

Letters poured in to the White House, mostly from children, after the puppies were born on Flag Day.

The First Lady heard of the letters from youngsters all over the country requesting

From Karen House

Dear Mr. President:

"I would like to have one of your pretty dog puppies. I would like a puppy so much because I never had a dog before and I like your dog verry (sic) much. If you give me a puppy I will be so happy.

"P. S. Write me back and answer my letter please Mr. Kennedy. I don't know how to spell the name of the dog that just had the babbies (sic)."

"Sincerely yours,
"KAREN HOUSE."

From Mark Bruce

"Dear Mrs. Kennedy:

"The other day I heard on the radio that the dog Mr. Krushev (sic) gave to you had pups and you didn't know what to do with them. On June the 8th I was playing baseball, I was batting. Our dog Midget got behind me when I was swinging the bat and I accidentally hit her in the head. She died almost immeditly (sic). I am a member of the Parkade 4 H. Midget was my project. I was in dog care. If you would let me have one of the pups I could continue in 4 H.

"The transportations may be a problem. My dad and brothers and few others boys will be going to Washington, D. C., for national R. A. congress. If you will let us have it they could pick it up.

"Thank you very much for your cooperation. Your friend,

"MARK BRUCE."

one of the puppies while she was in the hospital after the birth of Patrick Bouvier Kennedy, who died two days later.

She asked the White House correspondence section to pick 10 representative letters and send them to her. From the letters she selected the two children to be given the puppies.

Mark's appeal was based on the fact that his dog Midget had died "when I was swinging the bat and I accidentally hit her in the head." He told Mrs Kennedy that Midget was his "dog care" project in the 4-H and if he had one of the pups, "I could continue in 4-H."

With all of Pushinka's four puppies to be given away, the White House kennel of nine will dwindle to five — including Pushinka, Charlie, Clipper, a German shepherd, Shannon, a blue roan cocker spaniel and a gray Irish wolfhound, still not named.

Pushinka and Charlie's other two puppies—Blackie and White Tips—will be given away privately, Mr. Salinger said. One of the dogs already has been tagged for Sydney Lawford, 6, daughter of the President's sister Pat and actor Peter Lawford. The other puppy will go to an adult, Mr. Salinger said.

PRIZE PUPS—From the house where Lincoln lived, from the focal point of awesome Presidential power, from the mighty command post of the Western world—there will be sent forth today these two mewling puppies. They are the offspring of Caroline Kennedy's Welsh terrier Charlie and Pushinka, daughter of a Russian space dog, given the Kennedys by the Russians. And Miss Kennedy gave her blessing to the gifts to the two youngsters selected from the 5,000 letter-writing children who asked for the dogs, born on Flag Day. The story, and the texts of the letters written by the two children, page 4.

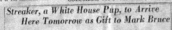

COLUMBIA DAILY TRIBUNE

Member of The Associated Press — COLUMBIA, MO., MONDAY, AUGUST 19, 1963 *PAGE ONE* PRICE 10c — FOUR

Streaker, a White House Pup, to Arrive Here Tomorrow as Gift to Mark Bruce

These two White House puppies, Streaker, a male, left, and Butterfly, a female, are on their way today to Mark Bruce, 9, of Columbia, 600 Karen House, 19, of Westchester, Ill. Streaker is scheduled to arrive here by air freight on an Ozark Air Lines flight scheduled to land at the Municipal Airport at 7:53 a. m. tomorrow. Streaker will leave Washington at five minutes before midnight tonight, Columbia time, on an Eastern Air Lines flight to St. Louis, arriving there at 3:29 a.m. He will be placed on the Ozark flight at 6:45 a.m. (CST). (Wirephoto)

Speechless when he first heard yesterday morning that the White House was sending him one of the puppies, Mark Bruce soon displayed a wide grin reflecting his happiness in receiving a replacement for his beloved pet, Midget. (Tribune photo)

For a growing boy like 9-year-old Mark Bruce, life has its moments of sorrow, of hope, of disappointment and of joy.

For Mark, son of Mr. Bert and Mrs. Byron Bruce of 706 Texas Ave., one of his proud moments came yesterday when he was informed by the White House that he will receive by air freight tomorrow morning one of the four puppies born June 14 to Pushinka, the daughter of Strelka, the Soviet dog that orbited the earth.

That moment of joy made up for the sorrow felt by Mark on June 9 when he swung a baseball bat during a neighborhood game without realizing that his pet dog, Midget, was behind him. The bat hit Midget and almost instantly killed her.

The moment of hope came June 19 when the Bruce family heard a newscast on KFRU indicating that the Kennedy family was undecided about what to do with Pushinka's puppies.

"Why don't you write to Mrs. Kennedy and ask her for one?" Bruce's mother suggested.

So Bruce took his pencil in hand and, on lined paper, wrote this letter to the First Lady:

"The other day I heard on the radio that my Mr. Khrushchev gave to you had pups and you didn't know what to do with them. On June the 8th I was playing baseball. I was batting. Our dog Midget got behind me when I was swinging the bat and I accidentally hit her in the head. She died almost immediately. I am a member of the Parkade 4-H Club. Midget was my project. I was to dog care. If you would let me have one of the pups I could continue to 4-H."

The letter ended: "Thank you very much for your cooperation. Your friend, Mark Bruce."

Within a few days Mark had a disappointing reply from Nancy Tuckerman, Mrs. Kennedy's social secretary.

"We were sorry to read of the accident to your dog, Midget," the letter said. "However, we regret that there are no puppies available for distribution from the White House.

But as time went on, youngsters from all over the country wrote to the Kennedy family asking for Pushinka's puppies.

Then, while Mrs. Kennedy was in the Otis Air Force Base, hospital recovering from the birth of a premature baby which lived less than two days, she asked to select some of the 1,000 letters requesting pups.

Among these, the First Lady chose Mark and Karen House, 19, of Westchester, Ill., to receive two of the puppies.

Both were notified by telephone calls yesterday morning from Mrs. Evelyn Lincoln, President Kennedy's personal secretary.

At the Bruce home the call came at about 9 a.m. after the Rev. Mr. Bruce and Mark's oldest brother, Ronald, 14, had left for an early service at the Memorial Baptist Church, where the Rev. Mr. Bruce is minister.

Mark answered the phone, and although the White House call had been placed for "Master Bruce," Mark misunderstood the long distance operator and believed the call was for "Mr. Bruce."

He called his mother to the telephone and she then talked to Mrs. Lincoln, who informed her that Mark would be given Streaker, one of the four pups and that his new pet would be air-freighted from Washington today.

"I can hardly believe it," Mark said. "I had prayed for another dog."

Mark, his mother, and his other brother, 12-year-old David, left shortly afterward for services at the Rev. Mr. Bruce's church, where members of the congregation soon learned of the White House call and congratulated Mark and the rest of the Bruce family.

The excitement continued as the Bruce home the rest of yesterday. Shortly after noon, news photographers arrived, long distance telephone calls kept the telephone ringing frequently as Mark was interviewed by wire services and radio and television networks.

"I almost hate to leave and miss the excitement," the Rev. Mr. Bruce said as he left early in the afternoon to conduct two wedding ceremonies, one at his church and one at Vandalia, Ill.

The exciting atmosphere was removed at about 9:30 this morning in the Bruce home when the Rev. Mr. Bruce received a telephone call from Pierre Salinger, the President's press secretary, telling him that Streaker will arrive on an Ozark Air Lines plane here at 7:53 o'clock tomorrow morning.

"The puppies are in good condition and are being prepared for shipment," Salinger said.

Early this morning, President Kennedy had flown back to Washington from Otis Air Force base with the two puppies aboard his jet plane. Also returning to the Capital with Kennedy, who spent an extended weekend of work and rest at Hyannis Port, Mass., were his two brothers, U. S. Sen. Edward M. Kennedy and Atty. Gen. and Mrs. Robert F. Kennedy.

After hearing of the gift of the puppy, Mark sat in the dining room of the Bruce home and began composing a letter of thanks to Mrs. Kennedy. Pictured with him are his parents, the Rev. and Mrs. Byron Bruce. (Tribune photo)

The President and Mrs. Kennedy are paying for shipping the puppies to Mark and to Karen. Karen's, a female, is named "Butterfly." She, too, will keep that name which was selected by President and Mrs. Kennedy's daughter, Caroline, who named all the puppies.

Mark said he plans to keep the name "Streaker" for his new male pet, which will sleep in the wicker dog bed he had required for Midget. "We already have some dog food."

"We're just a little bit nervous," Mrs. Bruce said. "We are so grateful to think we will have another dog."

The other two puppies, Blackie and White Tips. Also will be given away, but the Kennedy canine collection will still total five. In addition to the puppies' parents, Pushinka and Charlie, who is Caroline's Welsh terrier, the pets include Clipper, a German Shepherd, Shannon, a Blue Roan Cocker Spaniel, and a still unnamed Irish Wolfhound.

Also receiving one of Pushinka's puppies is Karen House, 19, of Westchester, Ill. Karen said she will keep the name "Butterfly" given to her pup by Caroline Kennedy. (Wirephoto)

(Continued on Page 3)

THE FIRST LADY'S CRISIS

Shortly after the flood of letters arrived at the White House, tragedy also visited. Even as I mourned the loss of my dog, the First Lady experienced her own, more serious crisis. President and Mrs. Kennedy were expecting their fourth child. Jackie's first pregnancy had ended in a miscarriage in August 1956. Their daughter Caroline was born in 1957, followed by John F. Jr., in 1960, and now a new baby was due on August 27, 1963. However, on the morning of August 7, Jackie began feeling the first stabs of labor pain. A helicopter flew her from their Squaw Island, Massachusetts, home to the Otis Air Force Base Hospital. At 12:52 p.m. doctors delivered Patrick Bouvier Kennedy by Cesarean section. They immediately placed the 4 pound, 10 ½ ounce baby in an oxygen-fed incubator. Patrick suffered from hyaline membrane disease (now known as neonatal respiratory distress syndrome), a lung condition that blocked the supply of oxygen to the bloodstream.[14]

The president arrived at the hospital at 1:30 p.m. Doctors recommended that he send his tiny son to Children's Hospital in Boston for treatment. Jackie never got to hold her newborn, only glimpsing him as her husband wheeled the incubator to her bedside before the ambulance's departure. When told that her son was being taken away, she was deeply distressed.[15] The baby never recovered, dying of cardiac arrest at 4:04 a.m. on Friday, August 9, 1963. He lived

14   Sally Bedell Smith, *Grace and Power: The Private World of the Kennedy White House* (New York: Random House, 2004), 393.
15   Smith, *Grace and Power*, 394.

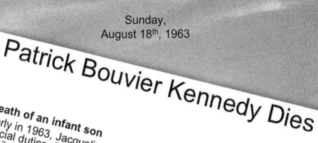

Sunday,
August 18th, 1963

Patrick Bouvier Kennedy Dies

Death of an infant son

Early in 1963, Jacqueline became pregnant again and curtailed her official duties. She spent most of the summer in the Kennedy family's Cape Cod compound at Hyannis Port, where she went into premature labor on August 7, 1963. She gave birth to a baby boy, named Patrick Bouvier Kennedy, via emergency Caesarian section at Otis Air Force Base, five and a half weeks early. Because his lungs were not fully developed, Patrick could not breathe and he was air-lifted to Boston Children's Hospital where he was placed in an oxygen-rich, pressurized room. He died of Hyaline Membrane disease (now known as Respiratory Distress Syndrome) on August 9, 1963. The couple was devastated by the loss of their infant son, and that tragedy brought them closer together than ever before.

only thirty-nine hours and twelve minutes after his birth.

A week after Patrick's birth, Jackie returned to their Hyannis Port home to recover. Convalescing from her Cesarean section and concerned about the growth of the pups and the overcrowding in the White House kennels, the First Lady asked her staff for a sample of ten letters from the thousands sent by people offering their homes for the pupniks.[16] Unbeknownst to me, my letter was one of the ten; it made the final cut.

And suddenly, my life changed.

THE PHONE CALL

On Sunday, August 18, 1963, my ordinary routine took an unexpected turn. Like any typical Sunday morning, Dad went to the church early to prepare for his two services. My oldest brother, Ron, went with him to participate in the youth choir. I was buffed and polished, ready for church, just waiting for Mom and my next older brother, David, to finish their grooming rituals. While I was waiting and reading the Sunday funnies in the kitchen, the phone rang and I answered. It wasn't unusual for the phone to ring on Sunday morning. Because of my mother's position as a Sunday School superintendent, teachers often phoned in sick or had last minute questions.

However, this Sunday morning I answered and heard an unfamiliar woman's voice on the other end. She politely asked for "Master Bruce."

16   Thomas, "Two Puppy Dreams Come True."

Around our house, I was not referred to as "Master Bruce." In fact, I had never heard of such a title except in the movies about slavery and the Old South. I thought this polite woman a bit eccentric, and that she must mean Mister Bruce. But why wouldn't she call my dad "Reverend Bruce," like everyone else? I informed the polite woman that he had already left for church and asked if she would like to speak to my mother.

"Yes," she responded, "that would be fine."

I handed the phone to Mom, who had arrived at my side by then. A several-minute-long conversation ensued.

Mom seemed more happy and animated than with most Sunday morning callers. Finally she said good-bye, hung up the phone, and turned to me. "Mark," she exclaimed, "you are going to get a dog from the White House!"

My immediate thought was: *Oh my gosh!* Then confusion: *But wait, hadn't they said they weren't giving any of them away? They must have changed their minds.*

The polite woman on the phone, who had identified herself as Evelyn Lincoln, President Kennedy's personal secretary, told my mother that the Kennedys had decided to give me one of the pups. Caroline Kennedy had named this pupnik Streaker. "Do you still want him?" Ms. Lincoln asked.

My mother quickly understood that when the president

Reverend Byron Bruce's
Church and family

offers to give you something, you don't say no, so she graciously accepted this gift on my behalf. Then Ms. Lincoln informed her that Mr. Salinger (Pierre Salinger, President Kennedy's press secretary) would contact us to provide additional details about Streaker's arrival.

Imagine having contact with the president's personal secretary! However, the renown of the people involved hardly registered with me. I was totally preoccupied with getting a new dog. Being ten years old, I hardly noticed the fact that the dog would come from the White House. Who cares about the White House when puppies are involved?

When we got to church, I asked Mom if I could find Dad between the two services and tell him the good news. With her permission, I waited in Dad's office for him to arrive. Somewhat surprised to see me, he must have known something was up. I relayed my wonderful news to him about getting a new dog.

He sat quietly and then asked how this came about.

I told him that the White House had called. "I guess they changed their minds, Dad. They're sending me a dog!"

I must put the next part of this story into perspective. We were Protestants, and the Kennedys were Catholics. We were Republicans, and the Kennedys were Democrats. We were an average middle-class, Midwestern family, and the Kennedys were rich, high society New Englanders. We had squeaky clean Midwestern values, and the Kennedys were, well, they were Kennedys.

Dad grasped this reality more than I did. Having experienced the vastness of the chasm between these two worlds, he couldn't easily accept that they could so effortlessly meet. In a dream, maybe. In reality, no.

I didn't have his historical experience, leaving me more innocent and more accepting. Some would call it naïveté, but I would also say that perhaps my pure and simple heart was more open to the loving touch of God. How often we miss His voice because we believe we know better!

Consequently, Dad and I didn't have the same perspective. He laughed and said somewhat condescendingly, "Mark, I think someone is pulling your leg. I think this is a very bad joke; I don't think you are getting a dog."

Those words stung a bit, and no amount of effort on my part could convince Dad otherwise. A media dispatch later quoted him as saying, "I thought he was fooling at first... All the boys at Sunday school were kind of envious of him this morning."[17]

I had to call on my mom to intervene. But by the time she came out of the office, Dad had also caused her to doubt the validity of the White House phone call just an hour earlier. Mom started worrying about what kind of scam this might be and how she could gently burst my bubble. Just two months before, I had been through a major childhood trauma, and now my relief had vaporized?

---

17   *"Caroline 'OKs' Gift of Puppies,"* Newark, New Jersey, August 19, 1963.

Mom couldn't focus on the church service that morning, her heart weighed down with what to do. However, my excitement continued to build as I eagerly awaited the arrival of my new dog. Perhaps I envisioned myself as David going forth to face Goliath, confident in the promise of God, much to the annoyance of his brothers. (Truth be told, my brothers acted similarly.)

When we made our way home from church, we found the phone ringing with the press wanting to talk to me. Peter Jennings, then a young reporter, was among the callers. The phone calls continued all afternoon, and photographers began to arrive. It became clear that the White House call was real, and I was finally getting a dog.

Dad was scheduled to officiate two weddings that Sunday afternoon. In the chaos of the moment, he left the house without his dress coat, and one of the reporters at the house actually took it to the wedding for him. At the Sunday evening church service, August 18, 1963, he told the parishioners that he was no longer Pastor Bruce, but "the father of the boy who was getting the dog from the White House." Although he didn't know it, reporters attended that service, and the quote appeared in the national papers the next day. We were overwhelmed by the press coverage and attention.

The next day, true to Ms. Lincoln's words, Pierre Salinger called to give us Streaker's itinerary. The pupnik would arrive by commercial airlines the next morning.

'Streaker' A
New Home
In Missouri

LAST WHITE HOUSE ROMP

WHY MY LETTER?

So how did I receive a dog even though I had been told the White House was not giving any away? It seems I had written before Jackie had come up with her essay contest plan. At that time they had no intention of giving the pups away. The idea of the contest only came when the First Lady realized that they couldn't keep all of the puppies because of the growing White House kennel population.

The WORD and WAY
White House Puppy: September 12, 1963
Delights Columbia Lad

Mark, ten-year-old son of Rev. and Mrs. Byron Bruce of Columbia, received one of the White House puppies. The other lucky person was Karen House of Westchester, Ill. Their letters were chosen out of 5,000 applicants for the puppies born to Pushinka, daughter of the Soviet space dog, Strelka. Pushinka was presented by Khrushchev to the Kennedys.

Mark had written, asking for a puppy, after his dog was killed in a baseball accident, and he was picked as Streaker's new owner.

The boy's father is pastor of the Memorial Baptist Church in Columbia.

And why did the White House staff choose my letter from among the thousands submitted? Perhaps because mine had arrived early, and those in charge decided it deserved first consideration, even though I didn't meet the guidelines for the contest. Certainly my letter addressed all the issues raised in the essay contest. I talked about how I would take care of the dog. And as a participant in the 4-H Dog Care Program, I would receive professional oversight.

Monday, August 19, 1963   THE WASHINGTON POST

WHITE HOUSE GIVEAWAYS: Streaker, left, and Butterfly, two of the puppies born to Pushinka, the dog given to Mrs. John F. Kennedy by Soviet Premier Nikita Khrushchev, have been cleared by Caroline Kennedy to go to Mark Bruce of Columbia, Mo., and Karen House of Westchester, Ill., respectively. The puppies are being dispatched by air to the lucky youngsters who will meet them at their local airports today.

Associated Press

After Caroline Gives Clearance

Two Puppy Dreams Come True

By Helen Thomas

HYANNIS PORT, Mass., Aug. 18 (UPI)—A 10-year-old girl in a Chicago suburb and a 9-year-old son of a minister of Columbia, Mo., got dream gifts today from President and Mrs. Kennedy—two of the puppies from the White House kennel.

Press Secretary Pierre Salinger said the First Lady had asked for a sampling of 10 of the 5,000 letters children had sent to the White House asking for the four puppies born June 14 to Pushinka, a mongrel, and Charlie, a Welsh terrier.

From those 10 letters, Mrs. Kennedy picked two to whom puppies will be sent.

These were Karen House, 10, of Westchester, Ill., and Mark Bruce, 9, of Columbia, Mo.

Karen is getting "Butterfly," a female and Mark will get "Streaker," a male puppy.

The President's daughter, Caroline, 5½, named all four of the brown puppies.

It was "cleared" with Caroline that all of the litter would be given away and she was "very enthusiastic" about the two puppies going to children who did not have dogs, Salinger said.

Salinger said Caroline also has agreed to let Karen and Mark change the names of the pets—if they want to.

THE TWO PUPPIES will ride back to Washington aboard the Presidential jet Monday when the President returns to the White House. They will then be shipped immediately to the eager children who know they are coming.

The dogs will be shipped to the children, complete with instructions on innoculations, and what they are being currently fed. Kennedy will pay the transportation costs, Salinger said.

Salinger said that Kennedy's personal secretary, Evelyn Lincoln, called both families today to tell them the ecstatic news. She first talked to Harold House, an air - conditioning salesman who called his daughter to

the telephone. Karen who had written the President that she "never had a dog before and I like your dog verry much" was "very excited" after Mrs. Lincoln called.

She also talked to Mark's mother, Mrs. H. Myron Bruce, wife of Rev. Bruce, pastor of Memorial Baptist Church.

Pushinka and Charlie's other two puppies—Blackie and White Tips — will be given away privately, Salinger said. One of the dogs already has been tagged for Sydney Lawford, 6, daughter of the President's sister Pat and actor Peter Lawford. The other puppy will go to an adult, Salinger said.

Again, I can only conclude that the God of heaven directed events with something greater in mind. Like my firm confidence when that initial phone call came through from the White House and all those who knew better doubted its legitimacy, I had a sense that my heavenly Father continued to watch over me. Faith told me that He continually acted in my best interest. I have experienced this many times since then. The One above hears my heart cry out when I have no one else to turn to, and I receive a response that can only be explained by the power of God. Some may call this coincidence. Some may dismiss it as a "hokey" belief in God with no grounding in reality. But I would beg to differ, having experienced the power and timing of the Almighty over and over.

FOR LUCKY KIDS — White House pups, Streaker (left) and Butterfly, are held by presidential aide Trephes Bryant in Washington. They'll go to Karen House (below) of Westchester, Ill., and Mark Bruce, Columbia, Mo. Mark is pictured at right with his parents, the Rev. and Mrs. Myron Bruce. (AP Wirephoto)

Chosen From 5,000 Applicants

Boy and Girl Will Get Pups From Pushinka

HYANNIS PORT, Mass. (AP)—A Missouri boy and an Illinois girl will get two direct-line descendants of the Soviet space dog Strelka from the White House kennel.

Mark Bruce, 9, of Columbia, Mo., and Karen House, 10, of Westchester, Ill., a Chicago suburb, expressed amazement Sunday when they learned that Mrs. John F. Kennedy had chosen them from among 5,000 applicants for puppies.

★ ★ ★

"I can hardly believe it," said Mark, a minister's son, who accidentally killed his dog with a swinging baseball bat this summer.

Karen said she originally got one of the standard White House letters rejecting requests for the pups because of the number of applications. But then came Sunday's telephone call from Mrs. Evelyn Lincoln, President Kennedy's personal secretary, and Karen said, "I'm all mixed up. I'm so happy."

Even her parents couldn't quite believe it—they called the White House to make sure it wasn't a prank.

★ ★ ★

Of the brown puppies born to Pushinka, daughter of the Soviet dog that orbited the earth, Karen will get Butterfly, a female. Mark will receive Streaker, a male.

Butterfly and Streaker, along with Blackie and White Tips, a gift to the Kennedys from Soviet Premier Nikita Khrushchev. The pups were sired by Charlie, Caroline Kennedy's terrier. Caroline named all four pups.

★ ★ ★

Karen House

Mrs. Kennedy, in a hospital recovering from the birth of a premature baby who lived less than two days, asked to see some of the letters requesting pups.

Ten were selected for her. From these the First Lady chose Karen and Mark to receive the puppies.

On lined paper, in pencil, Mark had written Mrs. Kennedy:

"The other day I hears on the radio that the dog Mr. Kruschev (sic) gave to you had pups and you didn't know what to do with them. On June the 8th I was playing baseball. I was batting. Our dog Midget got behind me when I was swinging the bat and I accidentally hit her in the head. She died almost immediately (sic). I am a member of the Parkade 4-H (club). Midget was my project. I was in dog care. If you would let me have one of the pups I could continue in 4-H. "Thank you.'"

The Flint Journal, Flint, Michigan

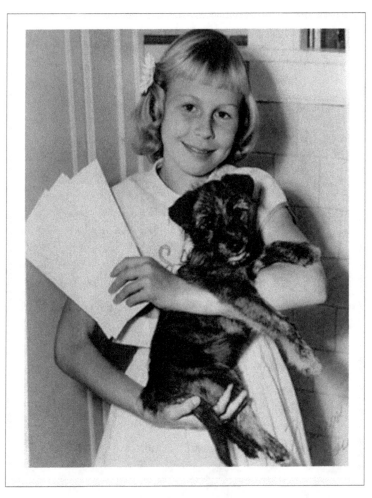

Karen House with Butterfly

Chapter Four:
Streaker

God continued to display His impeccable timing. The announcement about Streaker came at the beginning of a slow news week. Congress was in the middle of the August recess. The sad news of Jackie Kennedy's premature labor and baby Patrick's birth and death had passed, and the First Family was vacationing in Hyannis Port. The public no longer felt concerned about the Cuban Missile Crisis, and no one cared about the 1964 presidential campaign and election yet—except the Kennedys, of course. So when a White House press release came across the wires about presidential pups, the buzz-hungry press corps reveled in the chance for a feel-good story.

Mrs. Kennedy had decided to give away four of the famous pupniks. Two of the puppies would go to family members—including the president's niece, Sydney Lawford (daughter of the president's sister Patricia and the actor

Peter Lawford). But maybe even more newsworthy: The two winners of the White House essay contest would each receive one of the other two dogs from Pushinka's litter. A pupnik named Butterfly traveled to a girl in Chicago, and Streaker came to me![18]

New Ulm, Brown County, Minn.
Monday, August 19, 1963

NINE-YEAR-OLD Mark Bruce of Columbia, Mo., writes note of thanks to Mrs. John F. Kennedy, wife of the President, for selecting him to receive one of two puppies born to Soviet space dog, Strelka. Mark is shown with mother, Mrs. Myron Bruce. (AP Wirephoto)

The Austin Statesman
Wednesday, Aug. 21, 1963

UP AND AWAY—Butterfly, left, and Streaker, offspring of Caroline Kennedy's Welsh Terrier Charlie and Pushinka, daughter of a Russian space dog, are held aloft at the White House prior to departure for their new homes. The nine-weeks-old puppies were won   UPI Telephoto   by Karen House, 10, of Westchester, Ill., and Mark Bruce, 9, of Columbia, Mo., when their letters were selected at random by Mrs. Kennedy from about 5,000 sent to her and the President asking for Pushinka's puppies.

BUFFALO COURIER-EXPRESS, Wednesday, August 21, 1963

DOGGONE DELIGHTED—Mark Bruce, 10, hugs his gift puppy from the White House, Streaker, after the pup's arrival in Columbia, Mo., Tuesday. The pup is the second in a litter of four given away by the First Family to lucky youngsters.   AP Wirephoto

---

18   Thomas, "Two Puppy Dreams Come True."

THE NEW YORK TIMES, MONDAY, AUGUST 19, 1963.

White House Puppies Going to Midwest Children

By MARJORIE HUNTER
Special to The New York Times

HYANNIS PORT, Mass., Aug. 18—Two happy youngsters got the word today: they will receive White House puppies.

The puppies, Butterfly and Streaker, are part of the litter born June 14 to Pushinka, the dog given to the Kennedy's two years ago by Soviet Premier Khrushchev. The sire is another White House pet, Charlie, a Welsh terrier.

The choice of new homes for the brown pups was made by Mrs. Kennedy after sifting through some of the 5,000 letters received by the White House in recent weeks.

Butterfly, a female, will go to Karen House, 10 years old, daughter of Mr. and Mrs. Harold House of 1631 Hawthorne Street, Westchester, Ill., a Chicago suburb. Mr. House is an air-conditioning salesman.

Karen had written President Kennedy, asking for one of the puppies because she had never owned a dog. She confessed that she did not know how to spell the name of the dog "who just had the babbies."

Streaker, a male, will go to Mark Bruce, 9, son of the Rev and Mrs. H. Myron Bruce of 106 Texas Avenue, Columbia, Mo. The father is pastor of Memorial Baptist Church in Columbia.

Mark, in a penciled letter to Mrs. Kennedy, pleaded for a puppy to replace his own dog, Midget, whom he had accidentally killed while swinging a baseball bat.

Midget was his 4-H club project, Mark wrote, because "I was in dog care."

Mrs. Kennedy's decision to give away the two puppies was prompted by published reports that more than 5,000 children and adults had written to the White House asking for puppies.

At the time, Mrs. Kennedy

Puppies are shown by Traphes Bryant, White House aide

United Press International Telephoto
Mark Bruce

Karen House
Associated Press

was in the hospital at Otis Air Force Base, recovering from the Caesarean birth of a son, Patrick Bouvier Kennedy, who lived only two days. She asked to see some of the letters. After she received 10 of the letters from White House, she made her choices.

The 5,000 or so other persons asking for puppies have all been written to and told there are none now available.

The rest of the litter, Blackie and White Tips, will stay at the Kennedy home on Squaw Island for some weeks. They will eventually be given "to friends of the family," aides said.

Karen and Mark were tele-phoned this morning by the President's secretary, Mrs. Evelyn Lincoln, and given the happy news.

Butterfly and Streaker will accompany the President to Washington by jet tomorrow morning. There, they will be shipped by air freight to their new homes.

Mark, in his letter to Mrs. Kennedy on June 19, wrote:

"Dear Mrs. Kennedy:

"The other day I heard on the radio that the dog Mr. Khrushchev gave to you had pups and you didn't know what to do with them.

"On June 8, I was playing baseball. I was batting. Our dog Midget got behind me when swinging the bat and I accidentally hit her in the head. She died almost immediately. I'm a member of the Parkade 4-H. Midget was my project. I was in dog care. If you would let me have one of the pups I could continue in 4-H.

"The transportation may be a problem. My dad and brothers and few other boys will be going Washington, D.C., for National R. A. Congress.

"If you will let us have it they could pick it up.

"Thank you very much for your cooperation.

"Your friend, Mark Bruce."

Karen's letter, written in pencil on tablet paper, went to President Kennedy in late July. She wrote:

"Dear Mr. President. I would like to have one of your pretty dog puppies. I would like a puppy so much because I never had a dog before and I like your dog verry much.

"If you give me a puppy I will be so happy.

"P.S. Write me back and answer my letter please, Mr. Kennedy. I don't know how to spell the name of the dog who just had the babbies.

"Sincerely yours, Karen E. House."

NEW YORK POST, MONDAY, AUGUST 19, 1963

Khrushchev to Kennedy to Karen

Associated Press Wirephoto
Karen House, 10, of Westchester, Ill., (l) has been chosen to receive Butterfly, one of the four pups born to Pushinka, the space dog's offspring Soviet Premier Khrushchev gave to the Kennedy children. Mark Bruce, 9,
of Columbia, Mo., was chosen to receive a second pup, Streaker. In the center photo are Butterfly and Streaker. Karen and Mark were chosen by Mrs. Kennedy from more than 5,000 children who wrote asking for the pups.

First Lady's Choices   Richmond, Va

Boy, Girl Will Receive White House Puppies

New York Times News Service — HYANNIS PORT, Mass., Aug. 18—Two happy youngsters were informed Sunday they will receive White House puppies.

Butterfly and Streaker are part of the litter born June 14 to Pushinka, the dog given to the Kennedys two years ago by Soviet Premier Khrushchev. The father is another White House pet, Charley, a Welsh terrier.

The choice of new homes for the tiny brown pups was made by Mrs. Kennedy after reading 10 of the 5,000 letters of request received by the White House in recent weeks. Aides selected the finalists.

Butterfly, a female, will go to Karen House, 10, daughter of Mr. and Mrs. Harold House of Westchester, Ill., a Chicago suburb. House is an air-conditioning salesman.

Karen had written President Kennedy, asking for one of the puppies because she had never owned a dog. She confessed that she did not know how to spell the name of the dog "who just had the babbies."

Streaker, a male, will go to Mark Bruce, 9, son of the Rev. and Mrs. H. Myron Bruce of Columbia, Mo. The father is pastor of Memorial Baptist Church in Columbia.

Mark, in a penciled letter to Mrs. Kennedy, pleaded for a puppy to replace his dog, Midget, which he accidentally killed while swinging a baseball bat. Midget was his 4-H Club project, Mark wrote.

Mark Bruce

Karen House

(AP Wirephotos)

Streaker (left), Butterfly Will Start Journey to New Homes Today
About 5,000 Letters Requesting Puppies Were Received at White House

STREAKER'S ARRIVAL

Streaker arrived on Tuesday morning, August 20, 1963. I don't remember all the details of that day, but the myriad of news reports posted that week help fill in the blanks. Jim Lapham, writing for the newspaper *Kansas City* reported:

> As is their custom, Mr. and Mrs. Bruce got up about 6 o'clock this morning. Mark was sleeping. At 6:30 they got Mark up.
>
> "He wasn't hard to awaken this morning," his father said. And he was at the airport well in advance of Streaker's arrival.
>
> It was, Mrs. Bruce said, quite different from when Mark got Midget. That dog was the gift of Mark's 4-H leader and was given to him as a 4-H project. No fanfare marked its change of ownership.[19]

While I may not remember all the details, one memory is etched in my heart forever. I first met Streaker on the tarmac of Columbia, Missouri's municipal airport on that Tuesday morning. My family and I had arrived at the airport well in advance of the plane's arrival, not wanting to be late for such an auspicious appointment. Pressing myself against the outside of the chain-link fence around the tarmac, I

---

19   Jim Lapham, "Space Pup's Orbit in a Boy's Backyard," *Kansas City* (Kansas City, MO), August 20, 1963.

strained to see the dot in the sky that would be Streaker's plane. I didn't even notice the gathering of spectators and the press corps behind me. Would the moment of arrival ever come?

HAPPINESS—When the President's plane left Cape Cod today there were two puppies aboard—gifts from Mrs. Jacqueline Kennedy and Pushinka, the mother, who herself had been given to the President's family by Soviet Premier Nikita Khrushchev. About 5000 letters had poured into the White House asking for the pups. Two lucky youngsters got half of the litter—Karen House, 10 (left), of Westchester, Ill., who already has a picture of the pups, and Mark Bruce, 10, of Columbia, Mo., shown with his mother at right preparing a bed for his pet. President Kennedy will air freight the puppies to the kids at his own expense. Charlie, a Welsh Terrier and senior member of the White House Kennel, is the daddy. (Story on Page 7.)

Finally I saw the plane. With growing excitement I watched as the DC-3 landed and taxied to the tarmac where we were. The pungent smell of the plane's engines exhaust filled the air as the propellers stopped spinning. Once the cargo bay was opened and Streaker's shipping crate was removed, officials opened the fence gate for me. The passenger stairs were opened, but only a lovely stewardess descended and came to my side. The pilot restrained the rest of the passengers, but some peeked around the plane's door, no doubt wondering what was happening. My parents and brothers stood inside the fence, but not near me. This was my show.

At last someone brought the shipping crate over to me, and I opened it with the help of a baggage handler. When I took Streaker out of the crate planeside, he initially seemed a bit dazed. But he quickly warmed up to me, obviously delighted with human contact. And I was delighted with canine contact, especially after more than two months of loneliness. No question—I felt love at first sight.

Mark's Streak of Luck

It happened all because of Midget. Midget was a great dog; she was even helping her pal, 10-year-old Mark Bruce, with his 4-H project—dog care.

Then one day some of the fellows were playing baseball. Mark was at bat. He swung, not knowing Midget was near, and somehow the bat slammed against her . . . .

After Midget died, Mark, a busy Royal Ambassador and son of a Baptist minister in Columbia, Missouri, prayed for another dog.

Then he heard something on the radio one day in June—there were four new puppies in the White House kennel in Washington, D. C. Their parents were Charlie, little Caroline Kennedy's bouncy Welsh terrier, and Pushinka, daughter of the Russian space dog Strelka. Pushinka had come to America two years before as a gift to Mrs. John F. Kennedy from Soviet Premier Nikita Khrushchev.

Oh, how Mark would like to have one of those fuzzy little pups! He mailed a letter to Mrs. Kennedy, telling her about Midget and explaining that he wouldn't have to drop his 4-H project if he could have another dog.

Mark's letter even got in some free publicity for RAs. Worrying about how the puppy he wanted would get from the White House to 106 Texas Avenue in Columbia, he came up with an idea: Maybe his father and his two brothers—Ronald, 14, and David, 12—could pick up the dog while in Washington for the Third National Royal Ambassador Congress.

Then one happy August day a call came for Mark. It was from the White House. He was to get a puppy, brown with white-marked paws, named Streaker!

Another of the puppies, Streak-

Columbia Daily Tribune

Mark shows off his half-Russian friend, which used to live at the White House.

er's sister Butterfly, would go to live with 10-year-old Karen House and her parents in Westchester, Illinois. Karen, like Mark, had been one of 5,000 to ask for a pup.

When the news got around, things started hopping in Columbia! The phone jingled constantly;

news photographers kept popping up; letters streamed in from at least 20 states. Mark and Streaker even got their picture in *Life* magazine.

And that's how an RA got the grandson of a Russian cosmonaut for his best friend. ■

Streaker nuzzled me. He seemed to sense that he was home, and that I was going to take good care of him. That morning Streaker had been placed in a crate and flown from Washington, D.C. to St. Louis, where Ozark Airline personnel took him out of his crate for a brief period of time. From there he continued the short flight from St. Louis to Columbia. Did he feel a letdown when he had to transfer from Air Force One to an ordinary airliner? Certainly, his journey not only took him from Washington D.C., to Columbia, Missouri, but also from the heights of glory and power to my simple life.

𝔖𝔱. 𝔏𝔬𝔲𝔦𝔰 𝔊𝔩𝔬𝔟𝔢-𝔇𝔢𝔪𝔬𝔠𝔯𝔞𝔱   8-21-63

WHITE HOUSE PUPPY arriving in Columbia, Mo., responds enthusiastically to the warm welcome given him by his new master, 10-year-old Mark Bruce. The boy had written to Mrs. Kennedy asking for a puppy after his dog was killed in a baseball accident and the First Lady picked him as Streaker's new owner.   —A. P. Wirephoto

One of the flight attendants posed for photographs with me, as the airline passengers looked out from the opened aircraft stairway in delighted amazement. After the initial photo op, the plane's passengers were allowed to disembark although press cameras continued rolling.

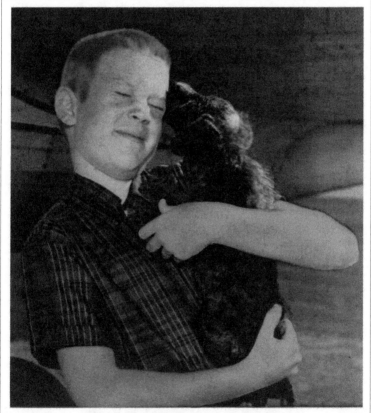

CLB 082001-8/20/63-COLUMBIA, MO. - Mark Bruce, 10, Columbia, greets Streaker, his new puppy - a gift of Mrs. Kennedy. Streaker, son of space dog Pushinka, arrived in Columbia this morning by airplane. UNITED PRESS INTERNATIONAL TELEPHOTO/gjb

Thursday
August 22, 1963   The Montgomery Advertiser

YOUTH GETS GIFT FROM JFK

Mark Bruce, 10, son of a Baptist minister of Columbia, Mo., is shown giving water to a new friend. The pooch was given to Mark by President and Mrs. Kennedy. The pup is a granddaughter of a Russian space dog which was presented to the President from Soviet Premier Nikita Khrushchev.—AP Wirephoto

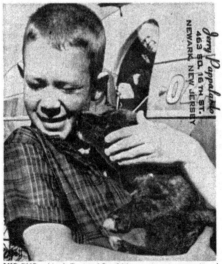

VIP PUP—Mark Bruce, 10, of Missouri, gets acquainted with Streaker, the gift of Mrs. Jacqueline Kennedy, at Columbia, Mo., Airport. Mark wrote asking for one of the pups of the Russian space dog, after his own dog was killed in an accident.

THE WHITE HOUSE
WASHINGTON

The pups should have their first permanent
live vacine on the 26th of August. They
should be fed three times a day (dog food is
PD -- three cans are included in this
package), about three-fourths of a can at
each meal. Also included with each meal should be
1/2 teaspoon of Vi-supple-min which is a vitamin
supplement. Besides this the pups can have
a little ceral and milk and cooked hamburger
each day.

The pups have been dewormed and treated for
hookworm. It is suggested that they be checked
again in two weeks.

THE WHITE HOUSE OFFICE

Mark Bruce
106 Texas Avenue
Columbia, Mo.

NEWS COVERAGE

While I was invested in nothing more than joyfully greeting my new canine companion, news reporters and photographers were focused on capturing it all with their notepads and cameras. This included a photograph of Streaker licking my delighted face. In short order, this sweet, unpretentious moment was published in newspapers around the world. It even merited a quarter page spread in the August 30, 1963, issue of *LIFE* magazine. And here all I had in mind was an affectionate moment with my new puppy!

Similarly, the photo which appears on this book's cover was published around the world by Associated Press International and accompanied many stories, including one by Jim Lapham, a staff reporter with the newspaper *Kansas City*.

> Streaker arrived at the Columbia airport shortly before 8 o'clock—an estimated six or eight pounds shipping weight. The Bruce family, Mark 10, and brothers Ronald, 14, and David, 12, and most of the neighborhood gang were waiting there.

> A few wholly-ignored passengers disembarked. All attention was focused on the baggage compartment to which Streaker had been relegated. A big white box was set on the ramp and the door opened on a sleepy eyed, fluffy black and brown 2-month old pup.

KANSAS CITY

KANSAS CITY, TUESDAY, AUGUST 20, 1963—28 PAGES

Ground Duty Is Ordered

Space Pup's Orbit in a Boy's Back Yard

By Jim Lapham
(A Member of The Star's Staff)

COLUMBIA, MO.—Space travel is too dangerous for his dog, young Mark Bruce said today without giving it a moment's thought.

Besides, Columbia has got a new leash law.

Space, for Streaker, probably will consist of the spacious back yard of the Rev. and Mrs. H. Myron Bruce.

Streaker arrived by plane this morning, the gift of Mrs. John F. Kennedy. The little dog is one of four pups born to the Kennedys' pet, P u s h i n k a, daughter of Strelka, the Russian canine cosmonaut.

Would he let the President borrow Streaker to send up in a space experiment, Mark was asked?

"No," was the immediate answer, accompanied by a vigorous shaking of the head.

Streaker arrived at the Columbia airport shortly before 8 o'clock—an estimated six or eight pounds shipping weight. The Bruce family, Mark 10, and brothers Ronald, 14, and David, 12, and most of the neighborhood gang were waiting there.

A few wholly-ignored passengers disembarked. All attention was focused on the baggage compartment to which Streaker had been relegated. A big white box was set on the ramp and the door opened on a sleepy-eyed, fluffy black and brown 3-month-old pup.

Both a Little Shy

Mark, a shy, quiet boy scooped up Streaker, a shy quiet pup, and cuddled him against his chest. Everybody else was excited.

Mark looked down and the pup tentatively licked Mark's chin. It tickled, but Mark only held Streaker closer. Finding Mark to his liking, Streaker set out to wash Mark's face for him, ending by burying his button nose in Mark's ear.

Streaker seemed as contented in Mark's arms as Mark was to hold him.

In addition to inheriting all of Mark's affection, Streaker gets

(Continued on Page 2.)

Proud owner and happy pup are Mark Bruce, 10, and Streaker, unlimbering his kissing apparatus for an airport greeting for his new master—(Kansas City Star photograph by Roger Reynolds).

tasty struck him with a base-ball bat this spring.

As is their custom, Mr. and Mrs. Bruce got up about 6 o'clock this morning. Mark was sleeping. At 6:30 they got Mark up.

"He wasn't hard to awaken this morning," his father said. And he was at the airport well in advance of Streaker's arrival.

Different Kind of Day

It was, Mrs. Bruce said, quite different from when Mark got Midget. That dog was the gift of Mark's 4-H leader and was given him as a 4-H project. No fanfare marked its change of ownership.

...rd

...om the White ...from a veteri ...Streaker's brief ...what vaccina-...given and what ...ed. Neither letter mentioned if Streaker was White-House-broke.

"At that age I'm sure he isn't," Mrs. Bruce sighed.

Pierre Salinger, presidential press secretary, in explaining that Streaker had received his name from Caroline Kennedy, said it would be all right if Mark wanted to rename the pup.

Mark said he didn't. Streaker suits him just fine. Everything about him is just fine.

But if President Kennedy wants to send a dog up in space he'll have to get himself another dog.

Mark, a shy, quiet boy, scooped up Streaker,
a shy quiet pup, and cuddled him against his
chest. Everybody else was excited.

Mark looked down and the pup tentatively licked Mark's chin. It tickled, but Mark only held Streaker closer. Finding Mark to his liking, Streaker set about to wash Mark's face for him, ending by burying his button nose in Mark's ear.

Streaker seemed as contented in Mark's arms as Mark was to hold him.[20]

Many stories like this one appeared in newspapers across the country. The whole world observed my innocent joy! They witnessed a young boy who loved dogs receiving a therapeutic balm that helped soothe the trauma from earlier that summer. Some reporters, hoping to have some fun with the situation, asked me whether I would allow the president of the United States to use my dog in NASA's space program experiments. My immediate and emphatic, "No!" brought on quite a chuckle.

The Columbia Daily, in its August 20, 1963 edition, recorded Streaker's arrival at the Bruce household in a story by Ron Walstrom:

The Rev. Mr. Bruce assured interviewers that Streaker "would just be a dog" in their home, primarily for Mark, "although I hope he will share it with us."

Later at home Mark's father shared he was

---

20   Lapham, "Space Pup's Orbit in a Boy's Backyard."

Vigorous Coexistence

Proud new buddy of a puppy, Mark Bruce, 10, ducks away from a licking at airport in Columbia, Mo. The pooch, Streaker, has just arrived from the White House. He's grandson of Soviet space mutt Ink.

DAILY NEWS, WEDNESDAY, AUGUST 21, 1963

New York Herald Tribune   Wednesday, August 21, 1963

'Streaker' Meets His Master

Mark Bruce clutching "Streaker" yesterday at the Columbia, Mo., airport.

COLUMBIA, MO. (UPI) Ten-year-old Mark Bruce and his White House puppy "Streaker" met for the first time yesterday. The dog, a gift from President and Mrs. Kennedy, arrived here by plane yesterday. Mark, his parents, The Rev. and Mrs. Byon Buce, and his two bothers, Ronald, 14, and David, 12, were on hand at the airport to greet the new member of the family. Streaker is from the recent litter of "Pushinka," the dog Soviet Premier Nikita S. Khrushchev gave to Mrs. Kennedy in 1961. Pushinka's mother was the Soviet space dog, "Strelka."

Mark wrote to Mrs. Kennedy asking for the puppy last June after his dog "Midget" was killed accidentally in a baseball game. Midget had been a 4-H project which he intended to enter in the Boone County fair. Another pup, a female, went to Karen House, 10, of Westchester, Ill.

not sure how big Streaker would get, but added, "I'm anxious to find out. It looks as if he will have long hair, though. That will help him withstand Missouri winters."

Streaker was placed in a wicker basket, at the Bruce residence, although he was soon out on the lawn, no doubt ready to have his feet back on solid ground after departing Washington, D.C., at 11:55 o'clock last night (Columbia time).[21]

---

21   Ron Walstrom, "Mark Bruce's Big Day Arrives, So Does Streaker—And It's Love at First Sight," *The Columbia Daily* (Columbia, MO), August 20, 1963.

THE COLUMBIA DAILY

VOL. LXII, NO. 289   Member of The Associated Press   COLUMBIA, MO., TUESDAY, AUGUST 20, 1963

Mark Bruce's Big Day Arrives, So Does Streaker — And It's Love at First Sight

"Streaker," until yesterday a resident of the White House, quickly made himself at home this morning after arriving at the residence of the Rev. and Mrs. H. Byron Bruce at 106 Texas Ave. Pictured with Streaker is Mark Bruce, who received the pup as a gift from President and Mrs. Kennedy. Streaker arived at the Municipal Airport from Washington shortly before 8 o'clock this morning. (Tribune photo by Earl Powers. For photograph of Karen House of Winchester, Ill., receiving Streaker's sister, "Butterfly," at Chicago last, night, see page 14.

Love at First Sight

(Continued From Page 1)

Streaker gingerly licked his new owner on the chin, cheek, ear and finger in a manner known only to a boy and his pet.

Even the pilots and stewardess paused to watch as Mark cuddled and fondled his new friend, who was shedding a little hair. Mark said little more than "yes" or "no" in answering questions at the airport. He seemed to have all a boy could want as he obliged photographers with wide grins.

The Rev. Mr. Bruce assured interviewers Streaker would "just be a dog" in their home, primarily for Mark, "although I hope he will share it with us."

Later at home Mark's father said he wasn't sure how big Streaker would get, but added "I'm anxious to find out. It looks as if he'll have long hair, though. That will help him withstand Missouri winters."

Streaker was placed in a wicker basket at the Bruce residence, although he was soon out on the lawn, no doubt ready to have his feet back on solid ground after departing from Washington, D. C., at 11:55 o'clock last night (Columbia time).

Neighbor dogs sensed a stranger and howled it up for a while immediately after the pup was home. The formal introductions will have to wait, since Streaker has been too young to receive some of his vaccinations. The Rev. Mr. Bruce said some of the inoculations will be administered Monday.

Streaker, a black and brown pup with white spots on his feet and a white streak on his nose, will be the first dog Mark has owned since his dog Midget was almost instantly killed by a baseball bat swung by Mark without knowing his dog was behind him.

Mrs. Kennedy picked Mark and a Westchester, Ill., girl to receive dogs from the Kennedy kennel. Both were among 5,000 writing letters requesting a pup.

Mark's brother Ronald seemed to sum it up for little brothers everywhere, including Mark, when he said, "We're all happy for Mark because sometimes he gets picked on."

Streaker may help to change that.

By RON WALSTROM
Tribune Staff Writer

LIFE on the Newsfronts of the World

The White House pups meet their adopters

It was puppy love at first sight. In Columbia, Mo. 10-year-old Mark Bruce (*far left*) grimaced with joy as a puppy named Streaker nuzzled his ear. In Chicago Karen House, 10, hugged a pup named Butterfly. The dogs were airborne gifts from the White House. Mrs. Jacqueline Kennedy chose Mark and Karen from 5,000 people who asked for the puppies, born to Pushinka, daughter of a Russian space dog, and Charlie, Caroline Kennedy's terrier. Who named the pups? Caroline, that's who.

After hearing of the gift of the puppy, Mark sat in the dining room of the Bruce home and began composing a letter of thanks to Mrs. Kennedy. Pictured with him are his parents, the Rev. and Mrs. Byron Bruce. (Tribune photo.)

Also receiving one of Pushinka's puppies is Karen House, 10, of Westchester, Ill. Karen said she will keep the name "Butterfly" given to her pup by Caroline Kennedy. (Wirephoto)

LIFE WITH STREAKER

Streaker and I bonded immediately. I loved him dearly and he loved me. We reveled in our shared and unconditional love. It didn't take long for Streaker to adjust to his new home and surroundings. His address may have been less prestigious than that of his previous residence, but his status had been greatly elevated. Rather than being one of nine dogs in the White House, Streaker became top dog in the Bruce household. He had my undivided attention. As I began the work of training, I felt an intense spotlight of self-scrutiny because of my accident with Midget. Similarly, my whole family had a heightened sense of vigilance with Streaker.

4-H was indeed valuable in helping me to care for and train Streaker. The dog care program included the basics of housebreaking, grooming, feeding, and obedience training. Just as I had done with Midget, we did leash training, off-leash training, and basic verbal and hand commands. With my family's support and aid, Streaker became an integral part of the Bruce household. When grown, he wasn't a large dog, about fifteen inches at the shoulder and around thirty-five pounds. He had an intelligent face and resembled a terrier. He was brown, had a prominent white streak on his nose (therefore his name), and had white socks. His name, somewhat a derivative of "Strelka," was an ever-present reminder of his lineage. I would always express thanks for this special dog to God, who saw my need and made this lofty provision.

Streaker and I had intense devotion to each other. Dogs have a hierarchy of loyalty within a household, and it became obvious that his allegiance belonged to me: I was his number one, his master. So whenever my brothers threatened me, they would first need to get by my dog. When my parents spanked me (which I deserved more often than I received), they first needed to take Streaker to another room. I gladly returned love to this brown-and-white pup, showering him with attention and affection.

First and foremost, my life suddenly revolved around Streaker. But as in any close relationship, both commitment and discipline must exist. Friendship requires a mutual exchange of love and affection, but always based on truth. Remove truth from the friendship and it will not last. And so it was with my friendship with Streaker—I had to train him. Training involves discipline, and I would cry whenever I needed to correct Streaker, whether in leash training or housebreaking. Mom always supported me in these times, knowing both the love and necessity of discipline in daily life. I realized the well-being of Streaker was at stake, including his life span and behavior well into the future.

HOMETOWN FAME

As I became a local celebrity for a few months, fan mail and even some hate mail started arriving at our house. Local TV shows asked me to appear on their programs, and I received invitations for interviews, photo shoots, and retail endorsements (really). Our little family, living at 106 Texas Avenue, acutely felt the attention of both locals and the media. Everyone wanted to be part of history in the making. Streaker and I received extensive coverage, and I carefully recorded the events and articles in a scrapbook. These were heady times for a boy of ten.

I remember the good times, but of course a puppy doesn't come into a household without causing some confusion. An article titled "Streaker Poses Many Problems," published in the *Columbia Missourian* some ten days after Streaker arrived into our household, reminds me of some of the difficulties Streaker caused.

> "The first few days were hectic," recalls Mrs. Bruce. "We got him [Streaker] early Monday morning, and though he slept that morning, he kept us awake that night. For the next day or so he kept me so busy, I didn't get the lawn mowed until Thursday."

> All last week, she said, various TV shows sought the services of "Streaker" and his master. The network "Today Show," televised the puppy's arrival into Columbia; the "emcee" of an eastern telecast "Wonderama" asked Mark and his pet to participate on his show; and the local "Captain Bob" show

had both on one of its programs:

"We've received letters from all parts of the country," Mrs. Bruce added, and the pile of mail on her desk showed.

"People have been very thoughtful," she said. "Many have enclosed clippings of how the story was run in their own papers. One lady—who was making a trip from New Jersey—stopped at numerous places on her way to Columbia to pick up different accounts of Mark's puppy and gave them to us. We've also received a memo from a Minnesota's congresswoman and a dollar bill from a student in Utah. That was to cover the costs of a photo he wanted of Mark and 'Streaker.'

"When people pass by our house, you can also hear some of them say, 'That's the dog.' Of course we've had many visitors stop in to see him too."

When visitors stop by they find "Streaker" to be a very active pup whose biting prowess would scare even the heartiest of postmen. "He bites everything," said Mrs. Bruce, pointing to one of her frazzled throw rugs. "See, he's just about ruined that rug."

Just then, the two-month old culprit scampered into the room and began to gnaw at Mrs. Bruce's shoe.

"No," she scolded him. "Not hard; don't bite hard."

Her son, Mark, added that "Streaker" also liked to gnaw at pillows as well as rugs and shoes. Mark said, the pup's favorite object seemed to the taped fly-swatter now lying at Mrs. Bruce's side on the floor.

"Yes, he's pretty active—and bites pretty hard," she grimaced.

"He likes to play and has investigated every part of the house. His favorite place, though, seems to be under the kitchen bar, wouldn't you say so, Mark?"

Mark belatedly nodded agreement. He was too intent on watching "Streaker."

"Mark," Mrs. Bruce yelled suddenly, "He's got Ron's collecting book." (Ron, 14, is Mrs. Bruce's eldest son.) Sure enough, "Streaker's" prey had switched once again—from the fly swatter to the collecting book.

Somewhat perturbed, Mrs. Bruce proceeded.

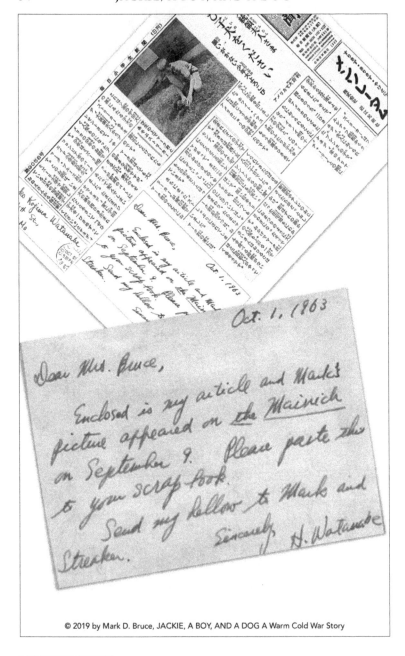

22   "Streaker Poses Many Problems," *Columbian Missourian* (Columbia, MO), August 29, 1963.

COLUMBIA (Mo.) MISSOURIAN, Thursday, Aug. 29, 1963—Page 17

'He Bites Everything'

Streaker Poses Many Problems

Ever since "Streaker" arrived 10 days ago, the family of the Rev. and Mrs. Byron Bruce, 106 Texas Ave., has been besieged by newspapers, television shows, callers and letters. All have congratulated the young pup's new master, Mark, and wanted to know more about his dog.

"Streaker," of course, is the brown puppy born June 15 to President Kennedy's Welch terrier and Pushinka, the offspring of the Russian space dog.

"The first few days were hectic," recalls Mrs. Bruce. "We got him early Monday and though he slept that morning, he kept us awake that night. For the next day or so, he kept me so busy that I didn't get the lawn mowed until Thursday."

ALL LAST WEEK, she said, various TV shows sought the services of "Streaker" and his new master. The network "Today" show televised the puppy's arrival into Columbia; the emcee of an eastern telecast called "Wonderama" asked Mark and his pet to participate on his show; and the local "Captain Bob" show had both on one of its programs:

"We've received letters from all parts of the country," Mrs. Bruce added, and the pile of mail on her desk showed.

"People have been v e r y thoughtful," she said. "Many enclosed clippings of how the story was run in their own papers. One lady—who was making a trip from New Jersey—stopped at numerous places on her way to Columbia to pick up different accounts on Mark's puppy and gave them to us. We've also received a memo from a Minnesota's congresswoman and a dollar bill from a student in Utah. That was to cover the costs of a photo he wanted of Mark and 'Streaker.'

"WHEN PEOPLE PASS by our house, you also can hear some of them say, 'That's the dog.' Of course, we've had many visitors stop in to see him too."

When visitors do stop by, they find "Streaker" to be a very active pup who's biting prowness would scare even the heartiest of postmen.

"He bites everything," Mrs. Bruce said pointing to one of her frazzled throw rugs. "See, he's just about ruined that rug."

Just then the two-month-old culprit scampered into the room and began to gnaw at Mrs. Bruce's shoe.

"No," she scolded him. "Not hard; don't bite hard."

HER SON, MARK, added that "Streaker" also like to gnaw at pillows as well as rugs and shoes. Mark said, the pup's favorite object seemed to be the taped fly-swatter now lying at Mrs. Bruce's side on the floor.

"Yes, he's pretty active—and bites pretty hard," she grimaced.

"He likes to play and has investigated every part of the house. H i s favorite place, though, seems to be under the kitchen bar. Woudn't you say so, Mark?"

Mark belatedly nodded agreement. He was too intent on watching "Streaker."

"MARK," MRS. Bruce yelled suddenly, "He's got Ron's collecting book." (Ron, 14, is Mrs. Bruce's eldest son.) S u r e enough, "Streaker's" prey had switched once again—from the fly-swatter to the collecting book.

Somewhat perturbed, Mrs. Bruce proceeded.

"Let's see," she mused. "He likes milk—especially when I pour syrup in it. When I do that, they say I'm spoiling him, but I keep him on dog food and I don't give him any table scraps though he loves hamburger and ham. Last Saturday evening, for instance, I gave him some hamburger and he didn't want his doog food for most of Sunday."

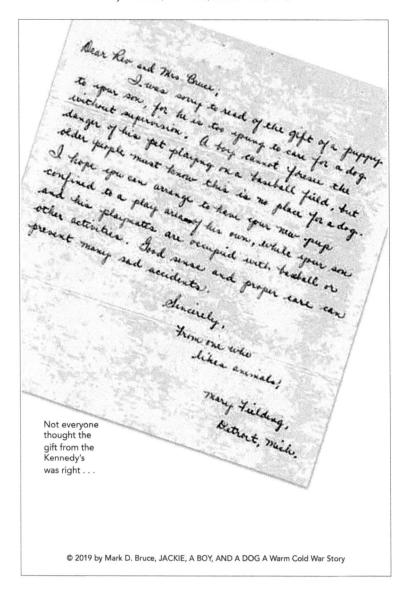

Dear Rev and Mrs Bruce,

I was sorry to read of the gift of a puppy to your son, for he is too young to care for a dog without supervision. A toy cannot replace the danger of his pet playing on a baseball field, but older people must know this is no place for a dog.

I hope you can arrange to have your new pup confined to a play area of his own, while your son and his playmates are occupied with baseball or other activities. Good sense and proper care can prevent many sad accidents.

Sincerely,

From one who likes animals,

Mary Fielding,
Detroit, Mich.

Not everyone thought the gift from the Kennedy's was right . . .

Slowly, I started to realize that Streaker and I had something special. We needed each other. But more than mutual need and affection, I became aware of Streaker's unique lineage, and that I had received a rare opportunity. I started to realize that the things that were happening to me were not happening to my friends, my classmates, my family, or anyone else in my circle of acquaintances.

I began to notice people treating us differently. Not just the press, but everyday friends and folks around town, began giving me and my family a sort of deferential treatment. I didn't think of myself as being "special," but clearly my life was different now and fame it had its effect, in ways both subtle and unsubtle. I was no longer anonymous. My parents and brothers kept me grounded in daily life—I was still a son and a brother. Yet now I had done things that others hadn't done: I had taken the initiative in a bold outreach that resulted in a sense of accomplishment. Humility didn't come easy for a ten-year-old boy who kept getting fan mail from around the country—even a newspaper clipping from Japan! But Mom and Dad kept me in place. I still had to do my chores around the house, wash the dishes, take out the trash, and weed the garden. My celebrity status didn't cut me any slack.

How could this be happening to me? Chance? Luck? Looking back, I have to believe that God intervened in my life and in my family's life—all for a purpose I didn't understand at the time. I had become the beneficiary of the most glamorous and famous lady in the world, but all I knew was that Streaker and I were made for each other.

CHAPTER FIVE:
THE
FIRST LADY

I knew little about Jacqueline Kennedy. In fact, I didn't actually care about who she was or what she represented. To me, she had importance simply because she gave me the puppy who became my best friend. But, even though I didn't realize it at the time, through my little brown-and-white ball of fluff, I became connected to someone in power. It was a connection that would last for many years to come.

LETTERS

It started with letters. Mom had written the Kennedys, expressing our family's gratitude for this gesture of grace. But because my parents had taught me good manners, I also dutifully wrote a note to the Kennedys, thanking them for the generous gift of Streaker. Much to my surprise, Mrs. Kennedy wrote back on September 3, 1963. The three-page handwritten letter read:

September 3

Dear Mark,

Thank you so much for your letter about Streaker.

I am glad you like him – and I think he is very lucky to have found a home with a boy like you who will love him and care for him –

Of all the puppies – he is the most like Charlie – the father – mischievous and loving to be with children. I hope this doesn't mean that he will grow up to be as disobedient as his father – who will never come when he is called –

But I am sure you will be able to take care of all of that in your 4-H class.

It made us all very happy to see that picture of you hugging him at the airport. Streaker is very lucky to be the only dog in a family that cares about him and to have you as his master –

We suddenly and unexpectedly find ourselves with lots of dogs – and one feels sorry for them, as it is hard to give enough affection to each –

Please do thank your mother for her very nice letter to me – I wish you all good luck with Streaker – You are lucky to have a mother who is so happy for you and doesn't mind the housebreaking problems that lie ahead –

All my very best wishes to you – and do let us know – my daughter will be very interested – how he turns out –

Sincerely,
Jacqueline Kennedy

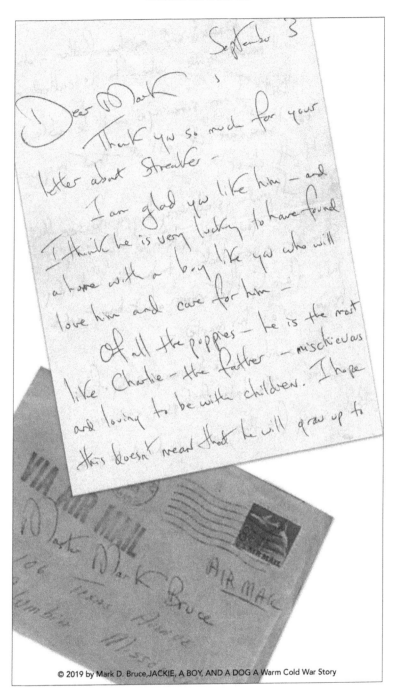

September 3

Dear Mark,

Thank you so much for your letter about Streaker.

I am glad you like him — and I think he is very lucky to have found a home with a boy like you who will love him and care for him.

Of all the puppies — he is the most like Charlie — the father — mischievous and loving to be with children. I hope this doesn't mean that he will grow up to

2)

be as disobedient as his father – who will never come when he is called –

But I am sure you will be able to take care of all of that in your 4-H class.

It made us all very happy to see that picture of you hugging him at the airport. Streaker is very lucky to be the only dog in a family that cares about him – and to have you as his master –

We suddenly and unexpectedly find ourselves with lots of dogs – and one feels sorry for them, as it is hard to give

3)

enough affection to each –

Please do thank your mother
for her very nice letter to me –

I wish you all good luck with
Streaker – You are lucky to have a
mother who is so happy for you and
doesn't mind the housebreaking problems
that lie ahead –

All my very best wishes to you – and do
let us know – my daughter will be very interested –
how he turns out – Sincerely.
                            Jacqueline Kennedy

The Bible story of the ten lepers Jesus healed comes to mind. Only one of the men who received healing came back to give glory to God. Only one came back to say, "Thank you!" The other nine missed out on something far more wonderful than their physical healing; they missed out on an encounter with God. And so it was with me. Through the gift of Streaker, I encountered God in a new way. He heard my heart cry and met my need, stirring up my heart of faith. Deep within myself, I knew I had received a touch from Him.

God also blessed me with something I didn't expect—my letter of thanks opened a doorway to a relationship with the First Lady of the United States. This friendship carried me through the next three decades, something I never imagined. She could have simply brushed me off as a completed project, a contact from the past. Instead, she took the time to reach out and make me feel important.

NOVEMBER 1963

Then, just two short months later, Mrs. Kennedy's whole world changed.

Most likely, every baby boomer can tell you exactly where they were on November 22, 1963, when they heard the news of President Kennedy's assassination. I remember sitting in class at Parkade Elementary School when the teacher told us the president had been shot. Like every other day, I walked home for lunch and there heard the news of his death on the radio. I first responded with disbelief. *How could this happen? Is Mrs. Kennedy okay?* Sadness and grief visited our home once again. Death always seemed to be just around the corner.

November 22, 1963
The presidential motorcade through Dallas a few moments before
President John F. Kennedy, 35th President of the United States, was shot.

Again Paul Harvey's voice became a pivot point as his noontime broadcast filled in some of the details of the president's assassination. As my family sat around the kitchen table eating lunch, we listened to the radio attentively—the same radio over which Mr. Harvey had asked, "What are they going to do with all those puppies?" during lunch a few months before. So much confusion surrounded the initial reporting, but one thing was clear: President Kennedy was dead. A young and dynamic world leader's life had been ended in an instant. As I walked the four blocks back to school, I noticed the trees, stark and bare of leaves, almost as if nature itself were mourning. I began to ponder the meaning of the tragedy and its consequences for our country, the world, and even myself. I hoped that President Kennedy had a real relationship to Jesus Christ, because there had been no opportunity for a "death bed confession" once the first bullet was fired.

The atmosphere back at school was somber. Some of the teachers and girl students cried. The magnitude of the tragedy began to sink into everyone's consciousness. I didn't cry; boys weren't supposed to cry. And after crying so much at Midget's death, I didn't think I had any tears left. But I was very sad. And I was aware that this was a loss, the effect of which would be far-reaching.

President Kennedy's death changed many things, of course, even for me. I never got to meet President Kennedy, but at the time of his death, I was expecting to. He had scheduled a campaign stop in Columbia in January, 1964, which was to have included a photo op with me and Streaker. Of course, this never transpired.

I also never met Mrs. Kennedy in person. Even still, she and I remained connected through letters. Of course, Mrs. Kennedy received an avalanche of mail after her husband's

death. One book recorded that she received over a thousand
letters of condolence and that people around the world sent
hundreds of letters to the State Department.[23]

Announcement from
Mrs. Kennedy in response
to a sympathy card from
Mark's mother.

It never occurred to me to send a sympathy card to Mrs.
Kennedy. However, my mother was one of those who expressed
her sympathy, and she received a card acknowledging her
kindness. Understandably, this acknowledgment was a
printed card from the White House, but my own letters to

23   Martin W. Sandler, ed., *The Letters of John F. Kennedy* (New York:
      Bloomsbury Press, 2013), 345.

Mrs. Kennedy in subsequent years were all acknowledged with a personal note and an expression of thanks. Now that I live in an age when most people correspond with messages sent by the touch of a button or the tap of a screen through social media, texts, instant messages, and e-mail, I marvel at the time she took to respond to me.

Through my ongoing friendship with the First Lady, I realized that she was a human who cared. Her own experiences of pain and horrendous calamity increased her compassion for others. I knew firsthand of her gentle spirit through her letters. While she could easily have dismissed me as an intrusion, she always expressed a genuine interest in my life. As I've grown into adulthood, my own journey from a naïve child to a busy and responsible adult has led me to especially appreciate the time she took to respond to me.

Tues., Aug. 18, 1964   St. Louis Globe-Democrat

AFTER A YEAR IN AMERICA, Streaker and Butterfly, grand-puppies of the Russian space dog Strelka, are happy pets in the homes of Karen House of Westchester, Ill., and Mark Bruce of Columbia, Mo. Both are 11 and were chosen by the White House to receive the dogs. Karen says "I love all animals, birds and fishes, but I love Butterfly the best." Mark told reporters, "Streaker chases a basketball around the yard and just keeps the family in stitches." —A. P. Wirephotos

In her first letter to me, the First Lady had written,

*"All my very best wishes to you — and do let us know —
my daughter will be very interested —
how he turns out."*

The Columbia
Missourian

People
and
Living

Section B—Sunday, August 16, 1964

Dog Days Are Here

(VERY IMPORTANT PUP) . . . Streaker, half Welsh ter, half Russian mutt, was born in the White House and to Columbia as a gift from Caroline Kennedy to 11-year-Mark Bruce, son of the Rev. and Mrs. H. Byron Bruce, Texas Ave. When Mark's former dog, Midget, was killed a accident last summer, the heart-broken boy wrote to John F. Kennedy, asking for one of the puppies of Caroline Pushinka, daughter of Russia's famous space dog, Strelka, a gift from Nikita Khrushchev. Father of the puppies was Caroline's Welsh terrier Charley. Mark's letter was chosen from hundreds received at the White House, and last Aug. 22 Streaker arrived, to fill an empty spot in the heart of a boy. The operation was a success, as evidenced by the picture above. Streaker is a prize pupil in Mrs. Pat Turner's obedience school, and boy and dog are inseparable. Mark has two brothers, David and Bob, but Streaker is a one boy dog.

© 2019 by Mark D. Bruce, JACKIE, A BOY, AND A DOG A Warm Cold War Story

I took her at her word. My very real friendship with Streaker spurred me on to communicate with Jackie Kennedy. We all like to connect with greatness, and we all like to have friends in high places, and that may have been part of my motive to write to Jackie, but I don't believe it was the primary one. Streaker's boundless love and faithfulness to me set the tone for my life, giving me a sense of genuine thankfulness that I wanted to express to the giver, the now former First Lady. And so I followed Jackie's suggestion by giving her an update every few years. As a testament to her character, she always wrote back.

© 2019 by Mark D. Bruce, JACKIE, A BOY, AND A DOG A Warm Cold War Story

A FAMILY MOVE

In 1966, our family moved from Missouri to Arizona. Streaker and his story followed me to our new home in Casa Grande. As I settled into my new life, an article in the local newspaper brought me disproportionate attention from the other students at my new school. By now, though, I was used to the recognition, accepting it as just a part of my life. I had developed a quiet confidence—not cockiness or arrogance—but a sense that I could do things other kids couldn't do.

After President Kennedy's assassination, I initially didn't know where to send my updates, so I would just send them to "Jacqueline Kennedy, New York, New York." In 1966 she sent a typed, but personally signed, letter:

September 26, 1966

Dear Mark,
I do want to thank you for your thoughtfulness in writing me all about Streaker and I am pleased to learn that he has been such a good friend to you these past years.

Caroline and John were delighted to see the picture you sent and it was most interesting to see what Streaker looks like now that he is no longer a puppy.

With appreciation for your kindness in writing and my very best wishes.

Sincerely,
Jacqueline Kennedy

September 26, 1966

Dear Mark:

I do want to thank you for your thoughtfulness in writing me all about Streaker and I am pleased to learn that he has been such a good friend to you these past years.

Caroline and John were delighted to see the picture you sent and it was most interesting to see what Streaker looks like now that he is no longer a puppy.

With appreciation for your kindness in writing and my very best wishes.

Sincerely,

Jacqueline Kennedy

Mr. Mark Bruce
1131 East 9th Street
Casa Grande, Arizona

Jacqueline Kennedy

Mr. Mark Bruce
1131 East 9th Street
Casa Grande, Arizona

Even in her letters, she had a way of making me feel that I was important to her. I could hardly believe it. She thanked *me* for writing *her*?

As I grew up, Streaker continued to play a major role in my life. My mother recalls times in Arizona when Streaker would accompany me and my brothers when we cleaned swimming pools for some of our church members. This activity would sometimes involve horseplay in the water, and Streaker would immediately begin barking at whomever seemed to be taking advantage of me. If the activity continued, he would jump into the pool and swim toward my attacker in my defense—a powerful deterrent to any bullying or horseplay.

Streaker also loved to ride in the car. We needed to be careful about using the phrase "car ride" around our house because when he heard those words, he immediately went to the garage door, anxiously waiting for it to open so he wouldn't be left behind.

© 2019 by Mark D. Bruce, JACKIE, A BOY, AND A DOG A Warm Cold War Story

Streaker knew exactly what presents were his at Christmas.

My next update to Jackie wasn't until I was a junior in high school, in May of 1970. My family had just moved from Casa Grande to Tempe, Arizona, where my father, who always preferred student ministry, had assumed the pastorate of a church in this university town. Jackie wrote back a typewritten note:

> *May 29, 1970*
>
> *Dear Mark,*
>
> *It was so thoughtful of you to write me all about Streaker. Caroline and John were so interested in the picture you sent and to learn about Streaker. From the photograph he looks like such a happy dog and I am certain this is due to all the love and attention you have given him over the years.*
>
> *I am glad your father likes his new position and perhaps one day we will all get to Arizona and see you and Streaker.*
>
> *Thank you again for writing me. It meant a great deal.*
>
> *Affectionately*
> *Jacqueline Kennedy Onassis*

I think my correspondence meant a lot to her; I believe these were not mere words. My connection with her had begun at a happier time in her life. It was a connection that happened through a higher power, a hidden Hand behind the scenes, perhaps bringing some small consolation to her broken heart. I hope I assisted in this process. I believe God led me, giving me the right words and intentions to help her healing. Who knows? I never had a chance to write to her about spiritual matters and the mercy God offers each of us, but I hope she recognized God's grace to her through our communications, the way I did. Although I never meant to impress Jacqueline, my love for Streaker compelled me to

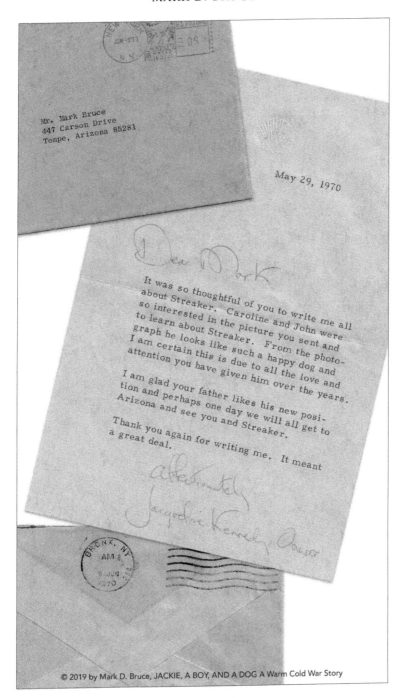

Mr. Mark Bruce
447 Carson Drive
Tempe, Arizona 85281

May 29, 1970

Dear Mark

It was so thoughtful of you to write me all about Streaker. Caroline and John were so interested in the picture you sent and to learn about Streaker. From the photograph he looks like such a happy dog and I am certain this is due to all the love and attention you have given him over the years.

I am glad your father likes his new position and perhaps one day we will all get to Arizona and see you and Streaker.

Thank you again for writing me. It meant a great deal.

Affectionately,
Jacqueline Kennedy Onassis

continue to express my gratitude to her and tell her what Streaker meant to me. Though we never met in person, I do believe her expressed hope of coming to Arizona with her children and seeing me and Streaker was genuine.

AUSTRIA

I was a good student in high school and enjoyed the sciences. In fact, just a few weeks after my letter to Jackie, I was selected as a summer program foreign exchange student to a province in southern Austria known as Carinthia. I was in Austria from the middle of June until September of 1970. I marvel at the evidence of divine intervention. Of all the countries in the world that I could have been assigned to, I ended up going to Austria, the genesis of my Streaker story. It was there that a conversation between the First Lady and Premier Khrushchev resulted in the Kennedys receiving Streaker's mother. My Austrian host, the Hans Kircher family, never knew of my celebrity, and it never occurred to me to bring it up, even though my relationship to Streaker had its roots in Vienna. I enjoyed the respite from all the attention, though I missed Streaker immensely.

My Austrian sojourn couldn't have been more perfect. The Kircher family farm is about 1,500 feet above the Drau River valley, on the slopes of the Alps. The main house on the farm is well over 300 years old. It was like living in a postcard. I helped out in the barn and in the fields, but mostly in the kitchen as a go-fer. Georg, the sibling closest in age to me, spoke the best English of the family. He worked as the waiter for the *Gasthaus* (inn) that the Kircher family also ran, and continues to run to this day. It was my first exposure to farm to table cooking, which was amazing. I quickly picked up the Carinthian accent and could communicate pretty well, although it certainly wasn't *Hochdeutsch* (High German, i.e., standard German). On Sundays the church bells would echo back and forth from the valley, calling the parishioners to worship. The Kirchers were Protestants, a significant minority in this predominantly Catholic society. Carinthia had actually been part of the Bible-smuggling route from Germany to Italy during the Reformation.

My time in Austria provided me with a dramatic change in life perspective. While overseas, one of my best friends died in a car accident. My parents and girlfriend informed me of the accident in a letter accompanied by a newspaper clipping with a picture of my friend's body covered with a plastic sheet. Again, I was to know grief. Even the natural beauty of the Carinthian Alps did little to assuage it.

But life moved on, and I had a duty to fulfill my exchange student commitment. I loved the Kircher family, and our mutual affection carried me through. Again, I was aware of divine intervention. I left Austria at the end of my twelve-week assignment, enlightened by the world beyond my life as an American boy. I also experienced spiritual growth and maturation.

Little did I know that after returning from Austria, another tragedy would strike.

Chapter Six:
Death
And Life

Being in Austria for twelve weeks tested my relationship with Streaker. We had never been apart for more than a few days, and I wondered if he would remember me. I had not been seriously homesick but actually missed Streaker as much as my family. I knew my parents and brothers would remember me, but would Streaker? Thankfully, my worry was unnecessary. We had a raucous reunion, reminiscent of our initial Columbia airport tarmac encounter.

However, just a few weeks after my return from Europe and being reunited with my own family and Streaker, I experienced another heartbreak.

TRAGEDY STRIKES

On a Sunday afternoon following a church service, my dad suffered a seizure. He had been having headaches, and these were occurring with increasing frequency. The seizure triggered a major diagnostic workup, including a brain biopsy, showing a glioblastoma, or brain cancer. The disease robbed my usually articulate father of his speaking ability. His words became confused and dysarthric—something incredibly frustrating for him to experience and painful for his family to watch. Miraculously, however, his speech had its familiar clarity when he prayed.

Dad died nine months later, shortly after my high school graduation. He left this world with grace and dignity, blessing me with a great heritage. To this day, I feel a void in my life. I miss him dearly, but know we will be reunited in heaven because of our trust in Jesus Christ as Lord and Savior.

Streaker was a great friend to me during this time, ever the unknowing consoler of a bereaved young man. I personally experienced the well-worn, but true, adage, "A dog is a man's best friend." The comfort that Streaker gave me can best be described as "ministry of presence." In a time of need, just having friends near—even canine friends—brings solace.

Death has a way of waking us up to the spiritual realm. How many times have I attended a funeral where I met people who suddenly took an interest in the reality of God—who, at least for a time, realized the human need to seek and find Him? Like a beam of light, death may rouse our hearts to pay attention to spiritual truths.

We all face death. First, we may make its acquaintance through the passing of our grandparents, then parents, and then perhaps siblings and friends. We cannot escape its reach. When it strikes, we are often inconsolable, not able to see beyond the power of its darkness. I had met death early in life when my first dog, Midget, died. Looking back, I can see that tragedy taught me that there is a way out. The God of all hope is worthy of my trust—He can make a way through grief, and He often uses those around us to help us through the darkness.

Jacqueline Kennedy Onassis became someone God used to help me through the difficult journey of grief. In my letter that prompted Mrs. Onassis's response in January 1972, I think I mentioned Dad's illness and death. I have wondered if my letters to Jacqueline were ever archived, but my search for them has not been fruitful. I can't help but think that her empathy was due to her knowledge of our family's sorrow. Her consolation to me after my father's death was important, reminding me to look upward and outward to the needs around me, for the world is full of hurting people, and we never know when our kind words will touch some wounded soul.

Jackie's own experience with death was a graphic one. News reports of that November day in 1963 tell that this fashion-conscious woman remained in her blood-spattered pink suit even as her husband was rushed to the hospital in Dallas and later flown back to Bethesda. Her journey with loss could have left her a bitter, self-pitying person, but she became armed with empathy, an empathy that touched me.

I will forever remember her kindness.

LETTERS DURING MY COLLEGE YEARS

Because of my father's sudden death, the summer of 1971 was a difficult one. After high school graduation, I enrolled in Mesa Community College to get my freshman year of English out of the way. The compressed summer school schedule allowed me to complete two semesters of English in a couple of months, leaving me with more time to focus on my premed studies in the fall.

My brother David had come home from his studies at Baylor University in Texas that spring to be with Dad during his illness. After our father died, David returned to school to continue his studies. I had also intended to go to Baylor, but with Dad's death, I was reluctant to leave Mom home alone.

I decided to live at home with Mom that year and begin my premed studies at Arizona State University (ASU). In fact, my mother and I both enrolled at ASU for the 1971–72 academic year. Years prior, Mom had completed two years of college but quit when she and Dad married. She had worked as a substitute teacher, and now she strove to finish a bachelor's degree in education. Mom and I often met on campus during the day. At night when we got home, we concentrated on our studies. Our busyness and academic challenges took the focus away from our heavy loss and helped us get through a very difficult time.

Streaker also helped me get through those dark days. His welcoming presence whenever I came home lifted my spirits. He always greeted me with barking, tail-wagging enthusiasm. My friendship with Streaker brought me comfort in a way I never felt with any other pet. We had other dogs, even while Streaker was alive, but none of them ever had my undivided attention. Streaker was special.

College was a challenging time for me, with academics calling for my full attention, and my Christian faith put to the test every step of the way. My parents had brought me up to trust in God and to seek to live in obedience to His will and ways. Now, as a young man, I sought to work this out in my daily life. The early 1970s presented real challenges to my Christian training. The popular notion of discarding all authority presented difficulties. Secular university life tested my beliefs. My science studies, with their emphasis on believing only in what we can see and touch, had an impact. I critically evaluated all the lessons I had learned growing up as my upbringing and values were put under a microscope.

Looking back, I now see my vulnerability. Thankfully, God's very real touch on my life through my parents and the gift of Streaker left a strong and unshakable imprint on my heart. My parents' godly example helped me plow ahead in this new world, and my relationship with Jackie encouraged me.

I sent her an update that year. I am not sure what I said in the letter, but it prompted Jackie to write an intimate letter back:

Jan 15 1972

Dear Mark,

The children and I were so touched to receive your letter about Streaker –

That was so kind and thoughtful of you to do – It was such a beautiful letter – I will keep it always –

You brought back so many memories of happy times long ago – I remember so well your first letter –

There could be no luckier dog than Streaker – to have spent his life with a master like you –

I can't believe that you are now in college –

With my best wishes for you always – and again, my deepest thanks – and all happiest wishes for the New Year

Affectionately,

Jacqueline Kennedy Onassis

Page 2 of January 15, 1972 letter from Jacqueline Kennedy to Mark

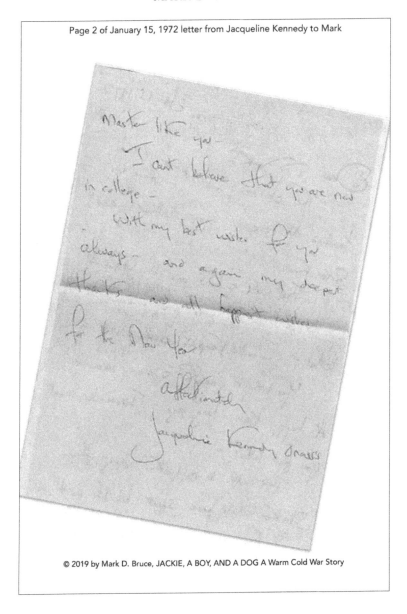

This is my most treasured missive from Jackie. Our pace of correspondence had increased to almost yearly, sometimes more. I kept these communications private, sharing them only with my family and a select group of friends. Streaker and Jackie were always in the background of my relationships.

My freshman year at ASU went by quickly. After spending a year with my mother, I discerned she was ready to be on her own, and I could pursue the next important step in my academic journey. I applied to and was accepted at Baylor as a transfer sophomore. In August of 1972 I moved to Waco, Texas, entering Baylor's premier premed curriculum. Although thankful I could spend more time with my brother David, who was still there, I was a little sad I couldn't bring Streaker with me to my dorm.

STREAKER BECOMES A FATHER

The big excitement in January 1973 was the birth of Streaker's pups, the next generation of pupniks. We mated Streaker with one of our other dogs, Nika, a Miniature Schnauzer. She gave birth to Heywood, Avis, and Churchill. Since I was home for the semester break, I helped birth them. One of the pups—Churchill—needed stimulation to breathe, and I was able to successfully resuscitate him. Mom kept Churchill, but because of his frailty, he lived only a few years. We never mated him. Heywood found a home with a family friend and lived to be ten or eleven, also without progeny.

January 1973
The birth
of Streaker's pups

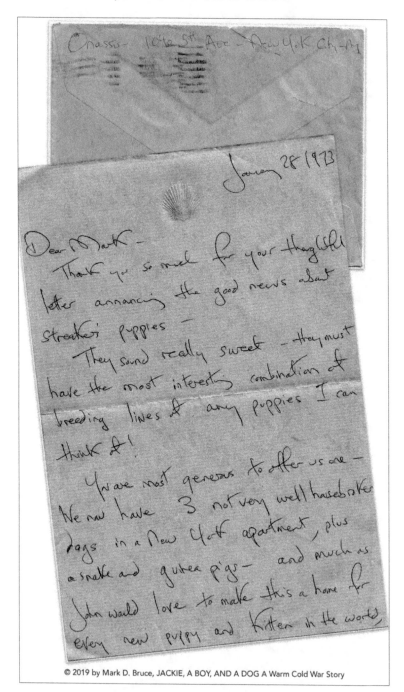

Onassis - 1040 5th Ave - New York City - NY

January 28 1973

Dear Mark -

Thank you so much for your thoughtful letter announcing the good news about Streaker's puppies -

They sound really sweet - they must have the most interesting combination of breeding lines of any puppies I can think of!

You are most generous to offer us one - We now have 3 not very well housebroken dogs in a New York apartment, plus a snake and guinea pigs - and much as John would love to make this a home for every new puppy and kitten in the world,

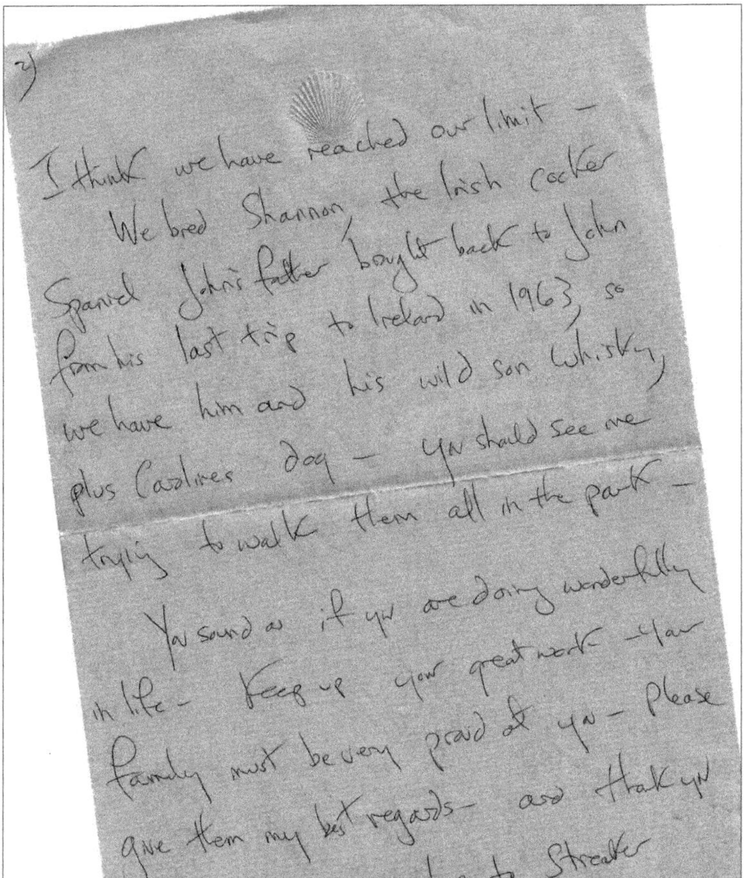

I think we have reached our limit —
We bred Shannon, the Irish cocker
Spaniel John's father bought back to John
from his last trip to Ireland in 1963, so
we have him and his wild son Whisky,
plus Caroline's dog — you should see me
trying to walk them all in the park —

You sound as if you are doing wonderfully
in life — Keep up your great work — Your
family must be very proud of you — Please
give them my best regards — and thank you
again — give my love to Streaker
all the best   Jacqueline Onassis

Mark Bruce
447 East Cassa Drive
Tempe

AIR MAIL

NEW YORK — PM 4 APR 1973

National Parks Centennial

I offered Avis, one of the pups, to Jackie, Caroline, and John. Jackie responded with a handwritten letter, with many personal details:

January 28 1973

Dear Mark,

Thank you so much for your thoughtful letter announcing the good news about Streaker's puppies –

They sound really sweet – they must have the most interesting combination of breeding lines of any puppies I can think of!

You are most generous to offer us one – We now have 3 not very well housebroken dogs in a New York apartment, plus a snake and guinea pigs – and much as John would love to make this a home for every new puppy and kitten in the world, I think we have reached our limit –

We bred Shannon, the Irish Cocker Spaniel John's father brought back to John from his last trip to Ireland in 1963, so we have him and his wild son Whiskey, plus Caroline's dog – you should see me trying to walk them all in the park –

You sound as if you are doing wonderfully in life – keep up your great work – Your family must be very proud of you – Please give them my best regards – and thank you again – give my love to Streaker.

All the best

Jacqueline Onassis

Evidently the above letter was misplaced because it wasn't mailed until April 4, 1973. In the interim, on February 23, 1973, Jackie wrote another letter regarding Streaker's pup, this one typewritten:

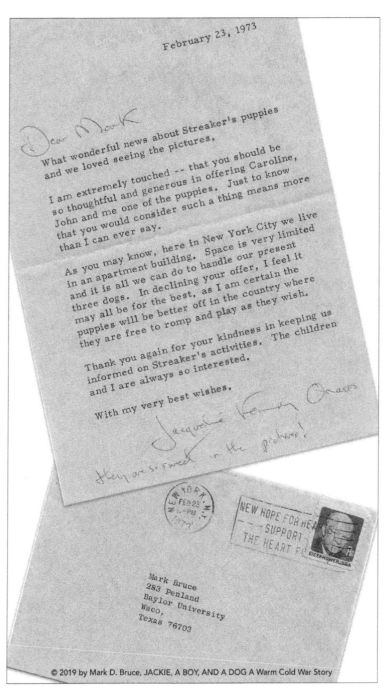

February 23, 1973

Dear Mark

What wonderful news about Streaker's puppies
and we loved seeing the pictures.

I am extremely touched -- that you should be
so thoughtful and generous in offering Caroline,
John and me one of the puppies. Just to know
that you would consider such a thing means more
than I can ever say.

As you may know, here in New York City we live
in an apartment building. Space is very limited
and it is all we can do to handle our present
three dogs. In declining your offer, I feel it
may all be for the best, as I am certain the
puppies will be better off in the country where
they are free to romp and play as they wish.

Thank you again for your kindness in keeping us
informed on Streaker's activities. The children
and I are always so interested.

With my very best wishes,

Jacqueline Kennedy Onassis

They are so sweet in the pictures!

NEW YORK N.Y.
FEB 23
6-PM
1973

NEW HOPE FOR HEA
SUPPORT
THE HEART F

EISENHOWER USA

Mark Bruce
283 Penland
Baylor University
Waco,
Texas 76703

February 23, 1973

Dear Mark,

*What wonderful news about Streaker's pup-
pies and we loved seeing the pictures.*

*I am extremely touched—that you should be so thoughtful and gener-
ous in offering Caroline, John and me one of the puppies. Just to know
that you would consider such a thing means more than I can say.*

*As you may know, here in New York City we live in an apartment
building. Space is very limited and it is all we can do to handle our present three dogs. In declining your offer, I feel it may
all be for the best, as I am certain the puppies will be better off in
the country where they are free to romp and play as they wish.*

*Thank you again for your kindness in keeping us informed on
Streaker's activities. The children and I are always so interested.*

With my very best wishes,
Jacqueline Kennedy Onassis
THEY ARE SO SWEET IN THE PICTURES!

Since Jackie didn't have room for one of Streaker's pups, I
offered Avis to my Baylor University physics professor, Dr.
Merle Alexander, who had been involved with the NASA
space program of the '60s and '70s. He was also very familiar
with the Soviet space program, the *Sputnik* flights, and even
knew about Strelka, Streaker's grandmother. He was *thrilled*
to get the pup! Avis, a wonderful pet for the Alexander
children, died without offspring when she was twelve. (By
the way, I also got an A in Dr. Alexander's class.)

I loved my years at Baylor. Unlike most premed students,
who usually majored in biology, I majored in chemistry.
My dad's illness and early death at age forty-five propelled
me toward a healthcare profession. I had felt so helpless
watching him fade away from his dynamic life and Christian
ministry. Separation from him by death was very difficult.

That experience taught me that death seems to come too early for some, and I wanted to be part of pushing back its boundaries. Thankfully, even though I still miss my father, I know our separation is temporary. Because of Christ's death and resurrection we will have a sweet reunion in heaven someday.

In 1973 my brother David graduated from Baylor and went to Duke Law School. Now on my own, and living off-campus, I had a sense of independence. I thought about bringing Streaker to live with me, but he was getting into his senior years, and I realized he'd do better with Mom and Nika in Arizona. So, I remained dog-less, except for going home at semester breaks. Our reunions always included displays of mutual affection.

In the spring of 1974, I let Jackie know that I was applying to medical school, with hopes for enrollment in 1975 after my Baylor graduation. She wrote a very supportive letter to me, delivered to my off-campus residence in Waco, Texas.

April 3, 1974

Dear Mark:

I was so pleased to hear from you again and the children and I love the pictures. It makes me so happy to know Streaker has given you such pleasure and I know what a wonderful home you have made for him.

How interested I am to hear that you may go to medical school. I do hope you will keep in touch and let me know your decision.

Once more, thank you so much for taking the time to write me. Caroline and John join me in sending you our very best wishes and regards to Streaker!

Sincerely,

Jacqueline Onassis

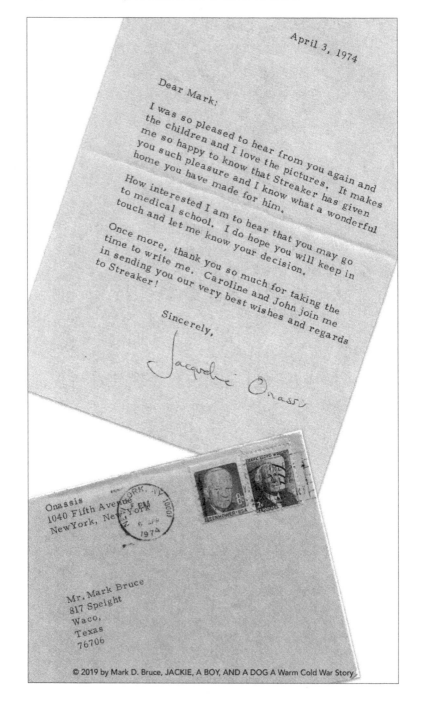

April 3, 1974

Dear Mark:

I was so pleased to hear from you again and the children and I love the pictures. It makes me so happy to know that Streaker has given you such pleasure and I know what a wonderful home you have made for him.

How interested I am to hear that you may go to medical school. I do hope you will keep in touch and let me know your decision.

Once more, thank you so much for taking the time to write me. Caroline and John join me in sending you our very best wishes and regards to Streaker!

Sincerely,

Jacqueline Onassis

Onassis
1040 Fifth Avenue
New York, New York

Mr. Mark Bruce
817 Speight
Waco,
Texas
76706

Applying to medical school is a very competitive process, with the very real possibility of not being accepted and then having to face the question, What do I do next? This was also the beginning of the affirmative action era, and I was a white male, middle-class kid. Furthermore, I couldn't use my connections to a former First Lady and a dog sired by a famous pupnik—application forms didn't allow me to boast in my affiliation with her either. I never thought to exploit my relationship with Jackie by asking for a letter of recommendation. Looking back, it may not have helped. With affirmative action, perhaps it would have even detracted from my cause.

All my initial med school applications were rejected. I had an interviewer congratulate me on my fine academic record, but tell me I was unlikely to be accepted because of my racial heritage and my gender—at least he was honest. The unfairness of this was particularly hard to swallow when I learned that one of the Hispanic students I used to tutor in chemistry at Arizona State University was accepted at the University of Arizona School of Medicine, while I was rejected.

I explored other options—a job offer from Exxon to work as a chemist and a possibility of working toward the Nuclear Propulsion Officer Candidate Program (NUPOC) with the US Navy. But in the end, I knew I didn't want to be a chemist or a nuclear engineer. I wanted to be a doctor.

Undeterred by the letters of rejection, I remained at Baylor, taking a few courses that interested me and establishing my Texas residency status. Like my experience when our household received the call from the White House that I was getting a puppy, I had a strong conviction to press forward with the plan to become a doctor. I believed God would help me. Some would describe this as instinct, but I would describe it as God whispering to me—calling me to the medical profession. God speaks and directs us in a variety of ways.

First, we come to know God's will by engaging in a personal relationship with Him. God has taken the initiative in this through the progressive revelation of His character in the Holy Scriptures, the Bible. He desires that we know Him. Because of God's holy and pure nature contrasted with our own sinful nature, we can only know Him through Jesus' sacrifice for our sins. God also knows us intimately, as we see in the words of King David in PSALM 139:13–16:

For you created my inmost being;
you knit me together in my mother's womb.
I praise you because I am
fearfully and wonderfully made;
your works are wonderful,
I know that full well.
My frame was not hidden from you
when I was made in the secret place,
when I was woven together in the depths of the earth.
Your eyes saw my unformed body;

all the days ordained for me were written in your book
before one of them came to be.

For you created my inmost being;

you knit me together in my mother's womb.

I praise you because I am

fearfully and wonderfully made;

your works are wonderful,

I know that full well.

My frame was not hidden from you

when I was made in the secret place,

when I was woven together in the depths of the earth.

Your eyes saw my unformed body;

all the days ordained for me were written in your book

before one of them came to be.

PSALM 139:13–16:

Second, we discover God's direction for our lives by paying attention to the natural talents and abilities He has given us. Recognizing what we are good at and what we enjoy will steer us toward certain vocations. The encouragement of others will also help us uncover the particular gifts God has blessed us with. I found that I was good at solving puzzles—that I liked science. My Baylor University faculty advisors boosted my confidence in this area. And Jackie's letters also encouraged me.

Truth be told, I couldn't bear to tell Jackie that I had been rejected and was giving up on my medical aspirations. And maybe a small part of me also felt Streaker would be disappointed in me if I abandoned my dreams.

We come to know God's will by engaging in
a personal relationship with Him.

We discover God's direction for our lives
by paying attention to the natural talents
and abilities He has given us.

© 2019 by Mark D. Bruce, JACKIE, A BOY, AND A DOG A Warm Cold War Story

Streaker, seventeen years old, with Mark's mom, Doris Bruce

CHAPTER SEVEN:
MEDICAL SCHOOL AND MARRIAGE

Thankfully, I never had to write a letter telling Jackie that I had not been accepted to medical school. God was gracious. When I reapplied to medical school, I was accepted at four schools (three in Texas, and one in Iowa). I returned home to Arizona to work for a few months in order to save up money for medical school. Mom was teaching fifth grade and had just completed her master's degree. We were both finding our way, step by step. I ended up committing to the College of Osteopathic Medicine and Surgery (COMS) in Des Moines, Iowa, now known as Des Moines University (DMU), College of Osteopathic Medicine.

I decided on COMS because of its three-year curriculum

(going to med school year-round for three years, without summer breaks) instead of the more traditional four-year curriculum. Since I had delayed my entry to medical school by one year, the three-year option appealed to me.

MEDICAL SCHOOL

Life in med school, especially in one with a compressed three-year curriculum, did not afford time to give attention to Streaker, who once again remained with Mom in Arizona. He was now thirteen years old or the equivalent of 65 in dog years. With all the news of Streaker, medical school, and my mother's advanced degree, I once again wrote Jackie in the spring of 1976, and she responded with congratulations and encouragement. Her response (typewritten and personally signed):

April 2, 1976

Dear Mark,

I was so pleased to receive your letter and we all love the picture of you with Streaker. He has the most appealing looking face and obviously you make him very happy.

Congratulations on being accepted at medical school. That is certainly a tremendous honor and you must be very proud of yourself. It is wonderful that you want to go into medicine and I wish you the best of luck always. Also, I think your mother completing her master's is a fine accomplishment, particularly since she is teaching at the same time. You are quite a family!

Again my thanks for writing and best wishes.

Sincerely,

Jacqueline Kennedy Onassis

Onassis - 1040 Fifth Avenue - NYC 100⸱8

April 2, 1976

Dear Mark:

I was so pleased to receive your
letter and we all love the picture of
you with Streaker. He has the most
appealing looking face and obviously
you make him very happy.

Congratulations on being accepted
at medical school. That is certainly a
tremendous honor and you must be very
proud of yourself. It is wonderful that
you want to go into medicine and I wish you
the best of luck always. Also, I think your
mother completing her master's is a fine
accomplishment, particularly since she
is teaching at the same time. You are
quite a family!

Again my thanks for writing and best
wishes.

Sincerely,

Jacqueline Kennedy Onassis

Mr. Mark Bruce
447 E. Carson Drive
Tempe,
Arizona 85282

The excitement of being accepted to medical school and the great optimism of becoming a doctor faded quickly as I faced the reality of the overwhelming lecture, lab, and study schedule. I also began wondering how on earth I would pay for medical school. Since my family did not have much in the way of financial resources, this training seemed almost beyond my economic reach. The US Navy came to my rescue with a health professions scholarship. This full scholarship included tuition, fees, and books, as well as a monthly stipend. In return, I had to commit to three years of active duty as a medical officer, upon completion of internship.

MOIRA

Medical school also brought someone new into my life. In Des Moines, I met Moira E. O'Brien—a fellow COMS classmate who became the love of my life. I first noticed this cute girl in shared lectures and at the cafeteria where she had a part-time job. We were very different: She liked to talk, and I was quiet and serious. Moira could sit at the back of the lecture hall, listen while she knitted, and remember every detail; I needed to sit in the front and take extensive notes so I wouldn't forget. Med school seemed to come easy to her; for me it was a struggle. But after about six months, I got up enough nerve to ask her out on our first date—a study break to eat at Poppin' Fresh Pies. We married during our second year of medical school, and afterward Moira also received a US Navy health professions scholarship.

When I first told Moira about Streaker, I think she doubted my sanity. But when I showed her the letters from Jacqueline Kennedy, she believed me and came to accept the "dog story" as part of my heritage. Through that boy-dog relationship, I had come to know unconditional love— perhaps a tangible picture of the unconditional love I had experienced through my relationship with Jesus Christ. Moira and I centered our marriage around Jesus Christ, not around each other, recognizing that marriage is sacred and a relational picture of Christ's love for the Church. We understood that love isn't simply a feeling—it's a commitment. Because of this understanding, my love for Moira has continued to grow over our forty-one years together and through the blessings of five children and seven grandchildren.

During our senior year of medical school, we did a six-month clinical rotation in Milwaukee, Wisconsin. While there, God gave us a passion for this area of the country. We knew we had an obligation to go where the Navy sent us after graduation, yet we hoped to return to Milwaukee someday.

In 1979, Moria and I both finished medical school. I invited Jackie to our commencement while also giving her an update on Streaker. She replied back in April 1979:

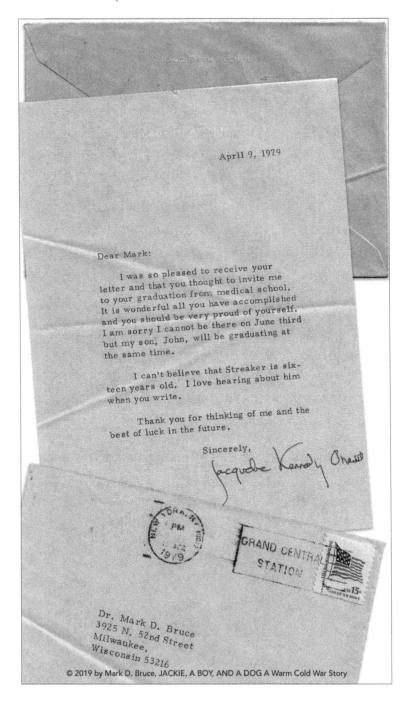

April 9, 1979

Dear Mark:

I was so pleased to receive your letter and that you thought to invite me to your graduation from medical school. It is wonderful all you have accomplished and you should be very proud of yourself. I am sorry I cannot be there on June third but my son, John, will be graduating at the same time.

I can't believe that Streaker is sixteen years old. I love hearing about him when you write.

Thank you for thinking of me and the best of luck in the future.

Sincerely,

Jacqueline Kennedy Onassis

Dr. Mark D. Bruce
3925 N. 52nd Street
Milwaukee,
Wisconsin 53216

April 9, 1979

Dear Mark,

I was so pleased to receive your letter and that you thought to invite me to your graduation from medical school. It is wonderful all you have accomplished and you should be very proud of yourself. I am sorry I cannot be there on June third but my son, John, will be graduating at the same time.

I can't believe that Streaker is sixteen years old. I love hearing about him when you write.

Thank you for thinking of me and the best of luck in the future.

Sincerely,

Jacqueline Kennedy Onassis

Mark and Moira Bruce

AFTER MEDICAL SCHOOL

After graduation, Moira and I moved to St. Louis for our postgraduate year of internship. If medical school was intense, internship was even more so. We began our postgraduate training at hospitals in St. Louis, representing a one-year detour from our active military service. This brutal year of internship became even more intense when Moira discovered a lesion on my neck that was diagnosed as melanoma. Since my dad had died of cancer, I can't say there wasn't fear attached to the diagnosis. Finding out you have a cancer is hard enough, but I suspect there may be an added level of trepidation when you've had a loved one taken by the disease. Thankfully, though, the melanoma on my neck was removed with surgery.

In 1979 Massachusetts Senator Ted Kennedy challenged President Carter for the Democratic Party presidential nomination. A press release announced that Jackie was coming to St. Louis for a campaign fundraiser for Senator Kennedy. Since Moira and I had a two-bedroom apartment, I figured we could host her overnight. So we sent Jackie a Streaker update, then extended an invitation for her to stay with us. She replied:

December 4, 1979

Dear Mark:

Thank you so very much for your letter and, as always, I am glad to hear about Streaker.

It is so very thoughtful of you and Moira to invite me to stay with you when I come to St. Louis, however, I have already made plans to spend the night with friends.

I am glad you are feeling well and trust you will not have any more health problems.

Sincerely,

Jacqueline Onassis

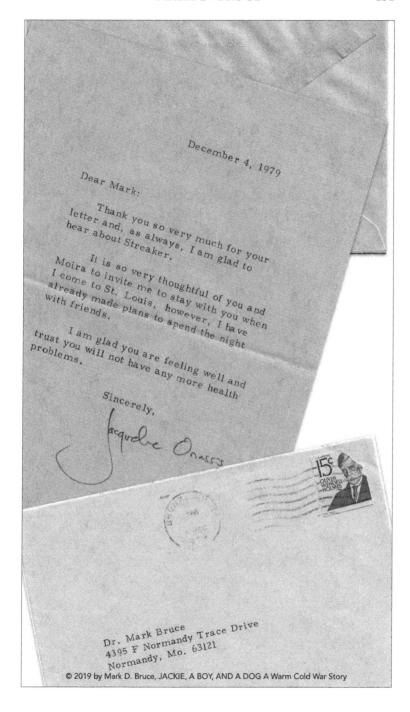

December 4, 1979

Dear Mark:

Thank you so very much for your
letter and, as always, I am glad to
hear about Streaker.

It is so very thoughtful of you and
Moira to invite me to stay with you when
I come to St. Louis, however, I have
already made plans to spend the night
with friends.

I am glad you are feeling well and
trust you will not have any more health
problems.

Sincerely,

Jacqueline Onassis

Dr. Mark Bruce
4395 F Normandy Trace Drive
Normandy, Mo. 63121

Jackie stayed at the estate of Kennedy family friends in the most exclusive area of St. Louis. I couldn't blame her.

LIFE IN THE NAVY

In July 1980, after our internship in St. Louis, the US Navy sent me and Moira to Camp Lejeune, North Carolina. Camp Lejeune is the home of the 2nd Marine Division, and, at the time, was also the location of one of the US Navy's Regional Medical Centers. I was stationed with the 8th Marines, part of the Rapid Deployment Force, as the Battalion Surgeon for the 1st Company. Moira was attached to the Naval Regional Medical Center at Camp Lejeune, as a staff physician in the Emergency Department.

The Navy scheduled me for an extended six to seven-month deployment to begin in February of 1981. However, shortly after we arrived at Camp Lejeune, Doug, one of my fellow 8th Marine Battalion surgeons, asked for my help. He and his wife had just had a baby, and he didn't want to leave his wife with a newborn at a military base far from home. He asked if I would be willing to switch deployments with him. The plan was for him to take my February 1981 deployment, and I would take his August 1980 deployment.

Moira and I discussed my colleague's request and decided to agree to it, not knowing that God's hand was very much in it. Still, it seemed logical. We had the happy news that

Moira was pregnant, but this deployment allowed me to return by the delivery date. The change of orders was submitted and ultimately approved.

The day I found out the new orders were approved turned out to be one of the saddest days of my life. My orders stipulated that I ship out in just a couple of weeks. I grieved the idea of leaving my wife, especially because that day I also learned that Moira had miscarried. The excitement and hope we felt with the news of the pregnancy was abruptly taken away. Moira and I knew all the medical reasons for this, but that knowledge didn't help in dealing with our sadness over what could have been.

The grief continued to pile up. That day my mom called to tell me that my good friend Streaker had died. My oldest brother, Ron, was dog sitting Streaker while Mom was in Illinois visiting her family. Mom had a fenced yard with a gate, but passersby often tampered with the gate. Evidently the gate was ajar, and Streaker, now mostly blind and hard of hearing, wandered out and into the street, where he was hit by a car. His injuries were extensive, and he couldn't be saved. I dutifully wrote Jackie about Streaker's death but got no reply prior to my embarkation. The local Phoenix newspaper, the *Phoenix Gazette*, commemorated Streaker's death in an article by staff reporter, Karen Fernau, on September 24, 1980:

Streaker's looks were deceptive. It wasn't

easy to tell that the scraggly, brown dog who had lived a quiet life in Tempe was famous from birth.

When Streaker died last month at the age of 17, a small chapter in history came to a close. But documentation of his life and how he eventually became the beloved pet of the A. Bryon Bruce family is still alive.[24]

The article went on to repeat the much publicized story of Streaker's heritage. It brought to a close a life well lived and one which I would fondly reflect on. It emphasized the special quality of Streaker, and my mom made this point when interviewed:

"When Streaker died, it was hard for me to tell my other two sons. We all loved him so much. But it was the hardest to tell Mark. There was just something between Mark and his dog Streaker."

Mrs. Bruce knows that Mark will eventually write Mrs. Kennedy one final letter to tell her that Streaker has died.

"I do not know if he has done this yet. It is so hard. Streaker was quite a dog."[25]

---

24 Karen Fernau, "Streaker's Story Will Never Die for Tempe Family," *Phoenix Gazette*, September 24, 1980.
25 Fernau, "Streaker's Story Will Never Die for Tempe Family."

Phoenix Gazette   Sept. 24. 1980

Streaker's Story Will Never Die For Tempe Family

By KAREN FERNAU
Gazette Reporter

Streaker's looks were deceptive. It wasn't easy to tell that the scraggly, brown dog who lived a quiet life in Tempe was famous from birth.

When Streaker died last month at the age of 17, a small chapter in history came to a close. But documentation of his life and and how he eventually became the beloved pet of the A. Bryon Bruce family still is alive.

So begins the story of Streaker:

The dog was born in June 1963 in the White House. John F. Kennedy was president. Streaker's mother, Pushinka, was a gift to Jacqueline Kennedy from Nikita S. Khrushchev, the Russian premier.

PUSHINKA WAS the mongrel offspring of the first Russian dog to orbit outer space.

Shortly after Pushinka gave birth to a litter of puppies, a tragic event happened to the Bruce family. It eventually resulted in a link to the Kennedy family.

"Our youngest son Mark was out in the backyard playing baseball and accidentally hit a ball that hit our dog Midget in the head. The dog died instantly. Mark was just heartbroken. He loved that dog," Doris Bruce said.

IT WAS HER suggestion that 10-year-old Mark write the Kennedy family and ask for one of Pushinka's puppies. Mark's heart-warming letter touched Mrs. Kennedy, who was in the hospital recuperating from the death of her infant son Patrick.

One Sunday morning that fall, Mrs. Bryon was getting her three sons ready to attend services at

DORIS BRUCE

Memorial Baptist Church in Columbia, Mo. Her husband, who was pastor of the church, had already left the house.

"The phone rang and I grabbed it, never thinking it would be someone from the White House. But it was John Kennedy's personal secretary. She asked if we were still interested in one of the puppies. I told her I was and she said that someone would call us on Monay to let us know when the dog would be arriving."

By Sunday afternoon the news media, hungry for a human interest story, had swarmed the Bruce household.

Turn to ● STREAKER, SE-2

● STREAKER — KENNEDY DOG

(Concluded from SE-1)

Streaker, who was named by Carolyn Kennedy, arrived the following Wednesday. The picture of the first jubilant meeting between Mark and the dog appeared in newspapers all over the world and in *Life* magazine.

Mark, who is now a doctor in the Navy, wrote a thank-you note to Mrs. Kennedy. Mrs. Bruce has kept the four-page letter Mrs. Kennedy sent back to Mark.

Mark and Mrs. Kennedy have written each other a short note every year since.

In each letter Mark has given her a report of Streaker.

"When Streaker died, it was hard for me to tell my other two sons. We all loved him so much. But it was the hardest to tell Mark. There was just something between Mark and his dog Streaker."

Mrs. Bruce knows that Mark eventually will write Mrs. Kennedy one final letter to tell her Streaker has died.

"I do not know if he has done this yet. It is so hard. Streaker was quite a dog."

FOR A 'DOG'S' LIFE —

His Life Story Impressive

by PAULETTE BOLYARD

If Streaker the dog could talk, he'd tell an impressive story.

He'd tell how he was born on Flag Day in 1963 in the White House and his first playmate was a little girl named Caroline Kennedy.

Because Streaker is proud of his family tree, proud enough to do some name dropping, he'd mention his mother Pushinka, offspring of the famous Russian space dog, Strelka. His father was Charlie, the First Family's Welsh terrier.

He'd go on to tell how he made a plane trip almost 17 years ago from Washington, DC to Columbia, Missouri to meet his new owner, Mark Bruce.

But Streaker doesn't talk, so it's Doris Bruce, Mark's mother and teacher at Kyrene Elementary School in Tempe, who does the reminiscing about Streaker.

"Mark was 10 years old then. We were living in Missouri. He was in 4-H and had a dog named Midget. She was his pet project for 4-H. It was the end of May or the beginning of June and Mark was playing baseball . . . ," she begins the account of the unfortunate accident that ended in Midget's death.

"Days later, after Midget's death," she skips forward, since the memory of the accident still hurts, "we were listening to Paul Harvey on the radio and he announced about four puppies born at the White House and he said, 'What are they going to do with four more dogs at the White House?' "

Mrs. Bruce mentioned to her son he might write and ask for the pups. So on his own, Mark wrote:

Dear Mrs. Kennedy:

The other day I heard on the radio that the dog Mr. Kruschev gave to you had pups and I was playing baseball. I was batting. Our dog Midget got behind me when I was swinging the bat and I accidently hit her in the head. She died almost immeditly. I am a member of the Parkade 4 H. Midget was my project. I was in dog care. If you would let me have one of the pups I could continue in 4 H.

The transportations may be a problem. My dad and brothers and few boys will be going to Washington, D.C., for National R.A. congress. If you will let us have it they could pick it up.

Thank you very much for your cooperation. Your friend.

Mark Bruce

"At first we got a letter back from the White House

Turn to Page 13

My deployment orders did little to assuage my grief and anxiety. The orders were cryptic, and it was not until we were in international waters on my ship, the USS *Saipan*, that we learned our mission was to invade Iran to rescue the American hostages held at the US Embassy in Tehran. However, our first order of mission was to participate in a NATO exercise in Norway, then go directly through the Suez Canal on our way into the Indian Ocean and the Arabian Sea.

After Norway, we came back for liberty in Portsmouth, England, and Moira came there to meet me. I had a very accommodating Navy Chief who gave me a week's leave to spend with Moira, even though this meant I would miss the ship's movement from Portsmouth to Lisbon, Portugal. Although this could have been a court martial offense, the officer covered for me. While with Moira, I learned Jackie had responded to my news of Streaker's death, and Moira shared the typewritten and personally signed letter with me. Jackie's letter reminded me I still had a friend, someone who knew my pain and cared.

September 10, 1980

Dear Mark,

Thank you so much for your letter telling me about Streaker. I know how much you must miss him, however, it should be of comfort to know that you gave him a long, happy life. I am so glad we sent him your way.

Good luck to you and Moira and I hope your cruise is a most successful one.

Sincerely,
Jacqueline Kennedy Onassis

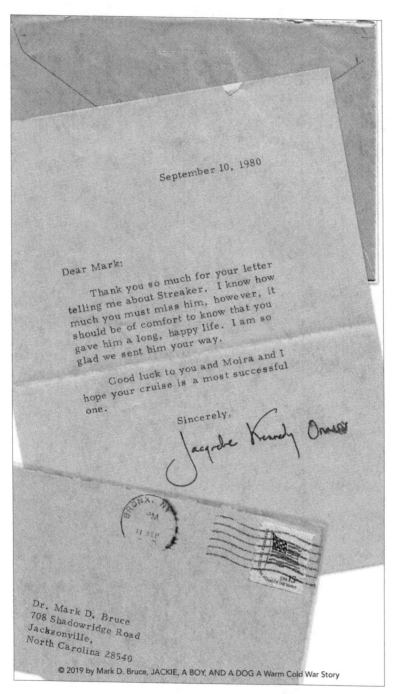

September 10, 1980

Dear Mark:

Thank you so much for your letter telling me about Streaker. I know how much you must miss him, however, it should be of comfort to know that you gave him a long, happy life. I am so glad we sent him your way.

Good luck to you and Moira and I hope your cruise is a most successful one.

Sincerely,

Jacqube Kennedy Onassis

Dr. Mark D. Bruce
708 Shadowridge Road
Jacksonville,
North Carolina 28540

During our time together, Moira and I ferried over to France, spending time with Jim and Diane Brower, friends of ours who were missionaries. After a week, Moira flew home and I hopped a train to Lisbon, where I met my ship. God was with us both, and I wasn't thrown in the brig.

The *Saipan* continued her journey with me again a part of the crew. After transiting the Suez Canal and going through the Red Sea, we stopped for fuel in Mombasa, Kenya. Leaving Mombasa, the *Saipan* experienced mechanical difficulties, which created problems with our invasion order. Ultimately the Navy canceled the order to invade because of the ship's difficulties, and because an investigative reporter had leaked the invasion plans. Our element of surprise was gone.

We reversed course and came back into the Mediterranean, stopping for liberty in Barcelona, Spain. Moira again met me there, and we spent most of the week in Sitges, Spain, an historic village on the coast, rumored to have been visited by the apostle Paul on one of his missionary journeys.Moira was pregnant again, with the pain and sadness of the summer of 1980 having largely passed. The remainder of the extended deployment went by quickly. After President Reagan was sworn into office, the hostages held for over four hundred days at the US Embassy in Tehran were released. We were briefly repositioned in the eastern Mediterranean as an option to receive the fifty-two hostages, but they were instead flown to Germany.

The final stop on this cruise was in Rota, Spain. Here the incoming Mediterranean fleet met up briefly with the outgoing US Navy 6th fleet, to be briefed on mission specific issues. I also met up with Doug, whose place I had taken, and who was now taking over my original assignment. We parted ways—I went home to Camp Lejeune and Doug began his Mediterranean duties. When I arrived back at base ten days later, I found many sad faces at my headquarters upon discovering the news that Doug had been killed in a helicopter crash during a military exercise on the coast of Spain.

Moira gave birth to David Jonathan at Camp Lejeune's Naval Regional Medical Center in June of 1981. We sent a birth announcement to Jackie, and she, of course, responded with hearty congratulations:

July 14, 1981

Dear Mark:

I was pleased to hear the news of the arrival of David Jonathan. You and Moira must be very excited to have a lovely, baby boy.

I hope your time in the Navy will go by swiftly and I wish you the best of luck in the future.

Sincerely,
Jacqueline Kennedy Onassis

In later years Moira and I sent birth announcements of our other children, but this was the last letter I received from Jackie.

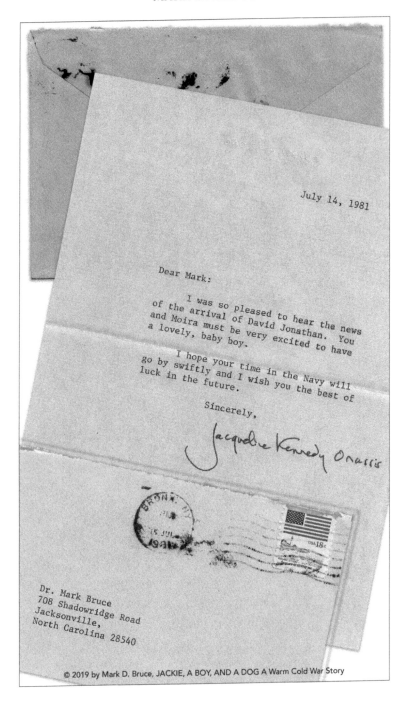

July 14, 1981

Dear Mark:

I was so pleased to hear the news of the arrival of David Jonathan. You and Moira must be very excited to have a lovely, baby boy.

I hope your time in the Navy will go by swiftly and I wish you the best of luck in the future.

Sincerely,

Jacqueline Kennedy Onassis

Dr. Mark Bruce
708 Shadowridge Road
Jacksonville,
North Carolina 28540

AFTER THE NAVY

Eventually, both Moira and I found the military lifestyle was not a good fit. Although grateful for the experiences we had, we longed to return to Milwaukee and put down roots. During my tour of duty, I found myself practicing emergency medicine and enjoying it immensely. I had originally planned to specialize in OB-GYN, but emergency medicine became my life's work. Moira had also

Dr. Mark D. Bruce

found emergency medicine to be a good fit for her, so we started pursuing our professional options in Milwaukee.

I found a professional home at Elmbrook Memorial Hospital in Brookfield, Wisconsin, now part of the Ascension–Wisconsin healthcare system, one of the largest faith-based healthcare providers in the world. I was the first board-certified emergency medicine physician there, and I eventually became both Chairman of the Emergency Medicine Department and the CEO of Brookfield Emergency Physicians, as well as Chief of Staff for the hospital. I was privileged to practice there for thirty-four years and oversee the development of a dynamic EM practice in the community.

We built a life in Milwaukee, eventually adding four more children to our family: Daniel, Timothy, Andrew, and Joanna. We found a church home in Brookfield at Elmbrook Church, a vibrant evangelical fellowship with excellent biblical teaching and a vision for worldwide ministry. There both Moira and I became involved with international ministry.

During those years I heard news that Jackie was ill with lymphoma. Her illness was private, but I intended to write to her and wish her well, to let her know that she was in our prayers. We did pray, but I didn't follow through with a letter.

Then, on May 19, 1994, Jackie died. She was surrounded by her family and friends. Our correspondence relationship had cooled due to busy schedules, family commitments, and long workweeks. Caroline and John received my condolence letter and replied with a printed general acknowledgment:

> *Thank you for your kind thoughts. Your support*
> *means a great deal during this difficult time.*
>
> Caroline Kennedy   John Kennedy

Jackie's life had ended, but for us, life continued. I had the privilege of serving on medical missionary teams in the Philippines and Indonesia. My biggest challenge in missionary medicine came after the December 26, 2004, tsunami. Relief workers in Banda Aceh, the island of Sumatra, Indonesia, asked me to mobilize a disaster relief team and come over to help. Banda Aceh was the first population center hit by the tsunami, killing an estimated 125,000 people.

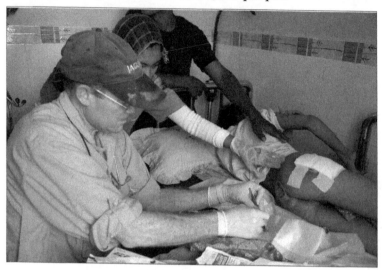

Dr. Mark D. Bruce serving with medical missionary teams.

The indigenous people often asked us, "Why are you here? You're Christian, and we're Muslims; you're supposed to hate us. You're rich and we're poor; why would you leave your home and come here?"

My response was, "I have experienced God's love and feel compelled to share it by putting my talents at His disposal."

They kept asking us to come back, and so for three years we did. I didn't look for this adventure; I merely walked through the door that God had opened. Our success in God's economy is not in any metric, like numbers of patients treated, or even diseases cured; it is in our obedience to His call.

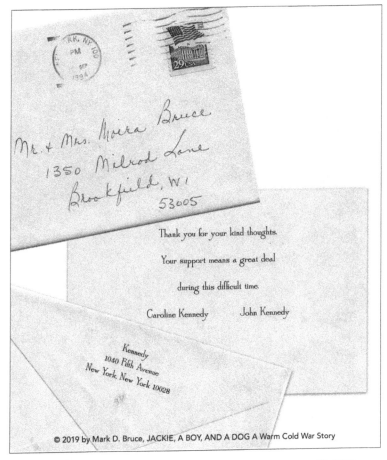

Thank you for your kind thoughts.

Your support means a great deal

during this difficult time.

Caroline Kennedy   John Kennedy

Kennedy
1040 Fifth Avenue
New York, New York 10028

Received after Jackie Kennedy Onassis passed away on May 19, 1994

I don't feel particularly gifted or unique, but I do have a willingness to allow God to use me. Jesus' choice of the disciples in the New Testament tells us this: God is looking for obedience. When we understand who are (sinners saved by God's grace) and who God is (the almighty, everlasting Creator of the universe), we can put our giftedness at God's disposal and let Him use us as He sees fit.

EPILOGUE

I stepped into the Great Gallery. Awed by the ostentatious dimensions, the massive crystal chandeliers, the artful wood inlaid floor, and the ever-present gilt, I remembered the events that happened in this room that changed world history and my little life.

Vienna had remained important to me over the years. I was eager to revisit the city where I had spent time in as a foreign exchange student almost four decades earlier, and especially looked forward to seeing the Schönbrunn Palace, a place steeped in history. Here the Ottoman Turks were repelled from their march into Central Europe in the Battle of Vienna. Here the royal Hapsburg family spent their summers. Here six-year-old W. A. Mozart played his first concert for Empress Maria Theresa, then ran and jumped into her lap, planting a big kiss on her face. As I strolled through the opulent rooms and grounds of the Schönbrunn palace, I thought about all that had happened in that magnificent setting.

But when I entered the Great Gallery of the palace, I contemplated how one conversation in that room had affected my own story. This grand chamber was the site of the legendary encounter between American President John F. Kennedy and his Soviet counterpart, Premier Nikita Khrushchev, during the 1961 Vienna Summit Conference. I could almost picture the charming Mrs. Kennedy making small talk with Khrushchev. I could imagine her not knowing what to talk about and finally landing on the subject of the space dogs, Strelka and Belka. I could almost hear her flippant, tongue-in-cheek suggestion that she would like to receive one of Strelka's new puppies.

And the rest is history.

GOD IS IN CONTROL

A visit to the Great Gallery not only taught me about the saga of important world events, but also made me ponder how God used an important meeting between world leaders to change the life of one young boy in Missouri—how God's hand in all of history reaches into our individual lives. God is in control of both the universe and the minutiae of our days. He works behind the scenes...yet deals with us on a personal level. He calls us to humility...yet allows us to be a part of His grand plan.

When I review my story of the intersection of a Russian space dog, a famous First Lady, and an ordinary Missouri boy, I can't help but be in awe of God, who controls all world events. In our careers, in the day-to-day busyness of our lives, we may be tempted to take credit for our successes and blame others for our failures. But the song "Who Am I" by Casting Crowns reminds me that I am not part of God's family because of who I am or what I've done. Instead it is only because of who Christ is and what He did for me that God says, "You are mine."

I have learned that I am not pulling the strings of my life. As the decades roll by, and I look back, I am struck that I am in a giant tapestry, put together by Someone else. I may think I am in control, but I truly am not. Someone outside of myself is nudging me in a certain direction, directing me along a path that I may be reluctant to choose. When we put our giftedness at God's disposal and let him use us as He sees fit, God amazes us with His plan. In the relinquishment of control, we gain freedom to be a blessing to a fallen world, to individuals in desperate need. Looking back, we see how God weaves events to guide us to His purposes and equips us to minister to others.

JEREMIAH 29:11 reminds me that God is in control:

> *"'For I know the plans I have for you', declares the Lord, 'plans to prosper you and not to harm you, plans to give you hope and a future.'"*

I still have a responsibility to develop my giftedness, but for His glory, not my own. I have great relief and comfort when I realize that I am called by the Creator of the universe, and that He has plans for me. We all have importance to Him. We are all loved by Him.

GOD WORKS BEHIND THE SCENES

Although God is control, He works behind the scenes. Have you ever thought about why the God who created the whole physical universe would also choose to be invisible to the naked eye? Our current culture teaches us to seek the physical, that which we can see and touch. Anything else is questionable, doubtful, or nonexistent. Too many of us accept that as true.

But my experience with Streaker and the First Lady helped me see a bigger world, a world where God orchestrated events to give me a dog when my heart mourned. I couldn't help but believe in a heavenly Father who, although hidden from our eyes, seeks to enter our lives if only we let Him. He doesn't push His way in. He doesn't insist we believe in Him. Rather, He is gentle and humble in heart and asks us to come and learn from Him (MATTHEW 11:28–29).

While much of His creation dismisses Him and carries on as if He doesn't exist, God remains patient in His love and grace. And just when we least expect it, He does something amazing and impossible, like sending a boy from Missouri a dog with a space lineage.

ISAIAH 40:28–31 speaks of how God, even in His majesty, gives relief where and when it is needed.

Do you not know?

Have you not heard?

The Lord is the everlasting God,

the Creator of the ends of the earth.

He will not grow tired or weary,

and his understanding no one can fathom.

He gives strength to the weary

and increases the power of the weak.

Even youths grow tired and weary,

and young men stumble and fall;

but those who hope in the Lord

will renew their strength.

They will soar on wings like eagles;

they will run and not grow weary,

they will walk and not be faint.

Even more, these verses remind us that His power enables us to rise above our circumstances.

GOD DEALS WITH US ON A PERSONAL LEVEL

Sometimes I wonder, Why did God arrange world events so I could have Streaker?

I have come to this conclusion: I was chosen to receive a pupnik dog because I have an assignment from heaven. God called me to tell the people of the world, now more than fifty years later, that the God of heaven cares for them.

When my heart was broken, I instinctively cried out to God because my parents consistently taught me that God hears my prayers. My parents didn't wait until I was in the middle of my crisis to prepare me for it. So I prayed with confidence for a remedy to my grief. We will all face crises. How we prepare for them is crucial. My former pastor, Stuart Briscoe, has said, "You can prepare for the inevitable, or not prepare for the inevitable. But the inevitable is inevitable." I am so thankful that my parents prepared me at an early age.

In his letter to the Philippians, the apostle Paul wrote,

> *Do not be anxious about anything, but in every situation, by prayer and petition, with thanksgiving, present your requests to God. And the peace of God, which transcends all understanding, will guard your hearts and your minds in Christ Jesus.*

We are commanded to present our requests to God! If God doesn't hear our cry for help, why would He command us to do this? The God of heaven is ready and waiting to respond to any person's cry for help. Who doesn't need help right now, as they watch world events and world powers spiraling dangerously out of control?

The God of heaven deals with us on a personal level, so personal that the Bible tells us,

> *"The very hairs of your head are all numbered."*
>
> (LUKE 12:7)

He also deals with us individually, according to our circumstances. No two of us are the same.

But He has also called us to testify to this experience of Him because after all, God is Spirit and we cannot see Him with our eyes. So I tell my story so others will know of His care and turn to Him. I can't help but talk about the God who healed my broken heart, and who continually seeks my betterment. Wouldn't you tell your friends if you knew something wonderful and beautiful that would benefit their lives?

GOD ALLOWS US TO BE A PART OF HIS PLAN

At times we may look at the chaos and destruction all around us and wonder how we can help. But surely the God of heaven who keeps the stars in their place and has ordered the physical world that we see each morning can lead us. He can help us to be part of the solution, and not part of the problem, as we move forward in our human existence. I'm in awe of how my heavenly Father orchestrated events in my life to connect me to a little dog and a famous woman and how those connections have given me opportunities to speak about His work in my life. I marvel at how He worked through the pain of my earthly father's death to lead me to a life of serving people in the medical field.

To think that God allows us to play a part in His plan

to bring His grace into this world amazes me. This has become my purpose, my passion, my reason for living. When I realize this privilege and responsibility, I cannot help but reflect on these verses:

> *For it is by grace you have been saved, through faith—and this is not from yourselves, it is the gift of God—not by works, so that no one can boast. For we are God's handiwork, created in Christ Jesus to do good works, which God prepared in advance for us to do.*

(EPHESIANS 2:8–10)

GOD CALLS US TO HUMILITY

My experience with the First Lady of the United States taught me a lot about humility. Jackie and I came from different worlds. A Catholic from high society—someone who knew wealth, pomp, and pageantry—reached out to a middle-class Protestant boy far from her life and existence. When I received the gift of Streaker, she made me feel important. When I sent her updates about the little dog she gave away, she could have brushed me off as a nobody. Yet she gave me her full attention by sending personal replies.

Even if we don't have the enormous weight of responsibility and sphere of influence that Jackie had, it's easy to dismiss those around us as intrusions on our resources and time. But Jackie's example inspired me as my own level of responsibility grew. The model of her kind replies motivated me as my influence and reach extended well beyond the sphere of that young boy in the summer of 1963. Now, as a physician at the top of the medical field, it's my job to give orders and see that things get done. If orders are not followed, people can die. But because of Jackie's example, I regularly pause to talk with the custodial staff as I stroll through my hospital, thanking them for their important work. They keep things sanitary and clean up the messes that I make. Sometimes it can be very unpleasant, but it is critical for the safe functioning of the hospital. I remind them of their tremendous worth. In some small way, I am continuing what Jackie did for me.

God tells us in His Word,

Humble yourselves, therefore, under God's mighty hand, that he may lift you up in due time.

(1 PETER 5:6)

If we are elevated to a higher position, let it be because of Him doing it, and not because of our own maneuverings. This is not an encouragement toward mediocrity or self-imposed lowliness and humility, but submission to heavenly principles that keep and guard our hearts.

My whole experience with Streaker reminded me that God arranged my life events, as painful as they were, to prepare me to receive that little pupnik. Through Streaker, I was elevated to a place to which I would not have been able to go on my own, and through Streaker's friendship, along with my parents' example, I learned all the principles embodied in a life of faithfulness and goodness.

GOD'S HAND SHAPES OUR LIVES

I see God's hand shaping my life, molding me into the man that He desires me to be. It started as a little boy when I accepted Christ's offer of redemptive love, knowing that I could never be good enough to merit God's favor and continued through the story I have recounted in these pages. The end result has been a meaningful life, lived to the best of my ability for the glory of God.

I am reminded of St. Paul's admonition in

1 CORINTHIANS 1:26–31:

Brothers and sisters, think of what you were when you were called. Not many of you were wise by human standards; not many were influential; not many were of noble birth. But God chose the foolish things of the world to shame the wise; God chose the weak things of the world to shame the strong. God chose the lowly things of this world and the despised things—and the things that are not—to nullify the things that are, so that no one may boast before Him. It is because of Him that you are in Christ Jesus, who has become for us wisdom from God—that is, our righteousness, holiness and redemption.

Therefore, as it is written: "Let the one who boasts boast in the Lord."

Like Strelka, who was a stray dog chosen for a special mission, I was nothing special. I just happened to have a love for dogs and baseball. And yet, through divine intervention, God moved the president of the United States and his wife to elevate me with the gift of Streaker. Out of tragedy came triumph.

THERE IS A GOD WHO CARES DEEPLY FOR EACH ONE OF US

Through this narrative, I hope not only to preserve a remarkable story of a First Lady, a boy, and a pupnik, but also to share the good news that there is a God who cares deeply for each one of us. Through the circumstances of our lives, He draws us closer to Him and then molds us and shapes our character. I recorded the lessons that God has taught me through this experience in hopes that they may have meaning for others. To God be the glory!

Now to him who is able to do immeasurably more than all we ask or imagine, according to his power that is at work within us, 21 to him be glory in the church and in Christ Jesus throughout all generations, for ever and ever!

immeasurably more

EPHESIANS 3:20.

APPENDIX 1:

GLOSSARY OF TERMS

THE COLD WAR

The term *Cold War* describes the open yet constrained rivalry between the Soviet Union and the United States after World War II. Although weapons were rarely used, the Cold War was fought on political, economic, and propagandistic fronts. George Orwell first coined the term in an obscure 1945 article where he predicted a nuclear stalemate between "two or three monstrous super-states, each possessed of a weapon by which millions of people can be wiped out in a few seconds."[26]

American officials strove to contain the spread of communism and the power of the USSR (Union of Soviet Socialist Republics). To that end, the United States started an unprecedented arms buildup and the

---

26   The Editors of Encyclopaedia Britannica, "Cold War," *Encyclopaedia Britannica*, https://www.britannica.com/event/Cold-War.

government encouraged the development of atomic weapons like the ones that ended World War II. In 1949, the Soviets tested an atom bomb of their own. President Truman responded by announcing that the United States would construct an even more destructive atomic weapon: the hydrogen bomb, or "superbomb." Stalin of the USSR then began his own quest for this weapon.[27]

CUBAN MISSILE CRISIS

The Cuban Missile Crisis brought the Cold War closer to American shores. On October 14, 1962, the pilot of an American U-2 spy plane photographed a Soviet SS-4 medium-range ballistic missile being assembled for installation on the island of Cuba.

On October 16, President Kennedy learned about the situation and immediately formed an executive committee (ExCom) of advisors and officials in order to deal with the diplomatic crisis. For nearly a week, they debated their options, including a bombing attack on the missile site and an invasion of Cuba. In the end, Kennedy chose a more measured approach. He ordered the US Navy to establish a blockade of the island to prevent the Soviets from delivering additional missiles and military equipment, demanding that the existing missiles be removed.[28]

On October 22, 1962, Kennedy appeared on national television to tell Americans, "Within the past week, unmistakable evidence of offensive missile sites is now in preparation on that imprisoned island. The purpose of these bases can be none other than to provide a nuclear strike capability against the Western Hemisphere."[29]

27   "Cold War," https://www.britannica.com/event/Cold-War.
28   History.com Editors, "Cuban Missile Crisis," January 4, 2010, https://www.history.com/topics/cold-war/cuban-missile-crisis#section_5.
29   Kenneth P. O'Donnell and David F. Powers with Joe McCarthy, *Johnny*

President Kennedy went on to describe his course of action against the Soviets.

Russian Premiere Khrushchev first replied that he had no intention of observing the American blockade and that the Russian vessels would not obey the stop orders from the US Navy. Kennedy and ExConn braced themselves for the approach of the Soviet ships. If shooting started at the blockade line, a nuclear war could quickly ensue. Everything came down to Khrushchev's reaction.

The Navy reported that two Russian ships, escorted by a submarine, were within a few miles of the blockade line. Tensions rose, but then another report came in that twenty Soviet ships had come to a stop before reaching the blockade line. Some were already turning around and returning to Europe.[30]

A deal ended the crisis. On October 26, Khrushchev sent a message to Kennedy offering to remove the missiles from Cuba in exchange for an American promise not to invade the island. The next day he also demanded that the United States remove its missiles from Turkey. Officially, Kennedy accepted the terms of the first message and ignored the second. But privately, the United States also agreed to remove the missiles from Turkey.[31]

The Cuban missile crisis demonstrated that neither superpower was ready to use nuclear weapons, because they feared retaliation and atomic annihilation. Both nations signed the Partial Nuclear Test Ban Treaty of 1963, banning above ground nuclear weapons testing.

We Hardly Knew Ye: Memories of John Fitzgerald Kennedy (New York: Little, Brown Publishers, 1972), 381.

30   "Cuban Missile Crisis," https://www.history.com/topics/cold-war/cuban-missile-crisis#section_5; O'Donnell and Powers, *Johnny We Hardly Knew Ye*, 384–385.

31   "Cuban Missile Crisis," https://www.history.com/topics/cold-war/cuban-missile-crisis#section_5.

LATER YEARS AND THE END OF THE COLD WAR

In the 1970s, Cold War frictions eased a bit with the Strategic Arms Limitation Talks (SALT) which led to the SALT I and II agreements of 1972 and 1979, where the superpowers set limits on antiballistic missiles and missiles capable of carrying nuclear weapons. Things heated up again in the 1980s, but by then the Soviet Union was starting to fall apart.

Soviet leader Mikhail S. Gorbachev began efforts to democratize the Soviet political system. Communist regimes in the Soviet-bloc countries of Eastern Europe fell. In 1989 the Berlin Wall was toppled and East and West Germany were reunited.[32] The Soviet empire was dismantled, and the United States became the reigning world power by default. The Cold War was over.

1961 VIENNA SUMMIT

On June 4, 1961, President John F. Kennedy of the United States and Premier Nikita Khrushchev of the Soviet Union met to discuss various issues between their countries. Their relationship began when Khrushchev sent Kennedy a letter on November 9, 1960, congratulating him on his victory in the United States presidential election. In continued correspondence, Khrushchev expressed a desire to negotiate with the United States on issues related to disarmament. On February 22, 1961, Kennedy suggested a face-to-face meeting and they agreed to meet in Vienna in June.

---

32   "Cold War," https://www.britannica.com/event/Cold-War.

ISSUES DISCUSSED

Berlin. Between the years of 1945 and 1961, 2.7 million Germans had emigrated from Soviet-controlled East Berlin to West Berlin (occupied by American, British, and French forces). East German officials wanted Khrushchev to close the border between East and West Berlin. Kennedy and Khrushchev debated the issue of a separate peace treaty with Berlin, something the United States did not want because then it could only communicate with West Berlin with permission from the East German government. This arrangement would therefore threaten the balance of power.

Laos. Khrushchev and Kennedy also discussed the situation in Laos, where the United States, during President Eisenhower's term, had backed a right-wing conservative government to prevent a communist threat. Both the United States and USSR wanted to avoid a proxy war in Laos, which would only further fuel an arms race.[33]

The Bay of Pigs. On April 17, 1961, a counter-revolutionary military group attempted to overthrow the government of Fidel Castro. This military group was largely made up of Cuban exiles who had traveled to the United States after Castro's takeover, but also included some US military personnel, trained by the CIA. The effort failed miserably, resulting in the capture of more than 1,100 men.[34] Immediately after the invasion began, Khrushchev sent Kennedy a message saying he was worried for the peace of the whole world. Kennedy thought it wise to meet with the Soviet leader as soon as possible in an effort to lessen conflict between the two superpowers.[35]

---

33   "Vienna Summit," https://en.wikipedia.org/wiki/Vienna_summit.
34   The Editors of Encyclopaedia Britannica, "Bay of Pigs Invasion," *Encyclopaedia Britannica*, https://www.britannica.com/event/Bay-of-Pigs-invasion.
35   "Vienna Summit," https://en.wikipedia.org/wiki/Vienna_summit.

RESULTS OF THE SUMMIT

Kennedy's advisors had counseled him not to take on his much more experienced counterpart so early in his presidency, but Kennedy felt his charisma could influence the Soviet premier, and diplomatic progress could be accomplished. However, Kennedy was unprepared for the pummeling he would receive from Khrushchev, who brought up the topic of war and drew him into a discussion of Marxism.[36] In the end, even Kennedy admitted he was outmatched. He told James Reston of *The New York Times* that the summit meeting had been the "roughest thing in my life." Kennedy went on: "He just beat the hell out of me. I've got a terrible problem if he thinks I'm inexperienced and have no guts. Until we remove those ideas we won't get anywhere with him."[37]

Just over two months after the summit, Khrushchev gave the go-ahead for the building of the Berlin Wall. And it is thought that his assessment of Kennedy's weakness and inexperience led to the Cuban Missile Crisis.

SPACE RACE

Between 1957 and 1975 the Soviet Union and the United States competed in the area of space exploration. It began with USSR's *Sputnik 1*, an artificial satellite launched on October 4, 1957, and ended with the Apollo-Soyuz Test Project human spaceflight mission in July of 1975. The race grew out of the arms race between the two countries after World War II when both nations acquired German scientists and advanced rocket technology.

---

36   A&E Television Networks, "JFK Was Completely Unprepared for His Summit with Khrushchev," History.com, July 13, 2018, https://www.history.com/news/kennedy-krushchev-vienna-summit-meeting-1961.

37   Nathan Thrall and Jesse James Wilkins, "Kennedy Talked, Khrushchev Triumphed," *The New York Times*, May 22, 2008, https://www.nytimes.com/2008/05/22/opinion/22thrall.html.

Because of their Cold War rivalry, the USSR and the US vied to be the first in launching artificial satellites, suborbital and orbital human spaceflight around the Earth, and in reaching the moon. These firsts were seen as indicators of technological and ideological superiority. The technology developed during the Space Race led to increased spending in education and research, as well as spin-off technologies that benefited the general public.[38]

SPACE DOGS

During the 1950s and 1960s, the USSR used dogs to test whether spaceflight was possible for living beings. Other animals were used as well, but the Soviets preferred dogs because officials felt they could endure long periods of inactivity.[39] They were also easier to train and readily available.[40] Because stray dogs would already be accustomed to harsh conditions, they were the animals of choice.[41] Training for the dogs included standing still for long periods of time and wearing space suits. The dogs were also placed in rocket launch simulators and centrifuges. They were fed a nutritious jellylike protein.

Between 1951 and 1960, more than twenty different dogs flew on eleven suborbital flights. Some of the dogs made multiple flights. In the early flights, the dogs wore pressure suits with acrylic glass bubble helmets. The animals were contained in pressurized cabins in later flights. Not all of the dogs survived.[42]

---

38   Wikia, "Space Race," http://military.wikia.com/wiki/Space_Race.

39   Wikipedia contributors, "Soviet Space Dogs," Wikipedia, The Free Encyclopedia, https://en.wikipedia.org/wiki/Soviet_space_dogs.

40   Richard Hollingham, "The Stray Dogs that Led the Space Race," BBC, November 2, 2017, http://www.bbc.com/future/story/20171027-the-stray-dogs-that-paved-the-way-to-the-stars.

41   Tony Long, August 20, 2010, "Aug. 20, 1960: Back from Space, with Tails Wagging," WIRED, https://www.wired.com/2010/08/0820sputnik-5-space-dogs-return/.

42   "Soviet Space Dogs," https://en.wikipedia.org/wiki/Soviet_space_dogs.

Laika was the first dog to fly in outer space. On November 3, 1957, engineers sealed Laika into the *Sputnik 2* space capsule, knowing she would never come back. Soviet leader Khrushchev ordered that a dog be flown by November 4, and in the hurry of the launch, no one had figured out how to get the animal back to Earth.[43]

On August 19, 1960, Belka (*Белка*, literally, "Squirrel" or alternatively "Whitey") and Strelka (*Стрелка*, "Little Arrow") spent the day in space aboard *Sputnik 5*. They traveled with a grey rabbit, forty-two mice, two rats, flies, and several plants and fungi. All survived. These *Sputnik* passengers were the first Earth-born creatures to go into orbit and return alive. After Strelka returned, she gave birth to a litter of puppies. One of these puppies was Pushinka, the dog Khrushchev gave to the Kennedys, and the mother of Streaker and Butterfly, the pupniks given to the winners of Jacqueline Kennedy's essay contest.

Other space dogs included Pchyolka, Mushka, Chernushka, and Zvyozdochka. Veterok (*Ветерок*, "Light Breeze") and Ugolyok (*Уголёк*, "Coal") spent twenty-two days in orbit aboard *Cosmos 110* from February 22 to March 16, 1966. They hold the record for the longest space flight by dogs.[44]

---

43   Hollingham, "The Stray Dogs that Led the Space Race," http://www.bbc.com/future/story/20171027-the-stray-dogs-that-paved-the-way-to-the-stars.

44   "Soviet Space Dogs," https://en.wikipedia.org/wiki/Soviet_space_dogs.

APPENDIX 2:

MEDIA COVERAGE

Friday, May 26, 1061
Toward Vienna

John F. Kennedy wanted a size-up, not a summit. And he had been wanting for a longer time than he had let on. Last week he made it official: on June 3, just after his visit to France's President Charles de Gaulle, President Kennedy will fly to Vienna for two days of informal, agenda-free talks with Nikita Khrushchev. Said the White House announcement, carefully worded to avoid raising any false hopes—or fears—of specific settlements: "The President and Chairman Khrushchev understand that this meeting is not for the purpose of negotiating or reaching an agreement on the major international problems that involve the interest of many other countries. The meeting will, however, afford a timely and convenient opportunity for the first personal contact between them, and a general exchange of views."

At first look. President Kennedy's decision to meet with Khrushchev seemed a hasty and perhaps dangerous effort to redeem recent U.S. failures in Southeast Asia, Cuba and other cold war hot spots. But, it now turns out, deep secret negotiations for the Kennedy-Khrushchev confrontation began a mere three weeks after Jack Kennedy's inauguration.

Before the Boiling. On Feb. 11, 1961—a time when the Congo was aflame but neither the Laos nor the Cuba crisis had yet boiled over—U.S. Ambassador to Moscow Llewellyn ("Tommy") Thompson was in Washington for top-level consultations on U.S. Russian relationships. He met lengthily in the White House with President Kennedy, Vice President Lyndon Johnson, State Secretary Dean Rusk, and three of his predecessors in Moscow: Averell Harriman, George Kennan and Charles Bohlen. The question of a Kennedy-Khrushchev meeting came up—and the consensus was that it might be worthwhile. Thompson returned to Russia with a Kennedy letter expressing hope for a meeting, possibly in ate spring, in a neutral European city. Thompson delivered the letter to Khrushchev in Novosibirsk, Siberia, on March 9 and got Khrushchev's "very favorable" response.

On March 27, Soviet Foreign Minister Andrei Gromyko went to the White House to see Kennedy, principally about Laos. Again the matter of a meeting of the two K's came up, and Kennedy said he was willing. Two weeks later, Khrushchev took visiting U.S. Pundit Walter Lippmann aside in the garden of a villa in Sochi and confided the news to him.

After the Fiasco. All that happened before the Cuba fiasco and the sudden collapse of the Western position in Laos. Then Jack Kennedy had more than enough to cope with. On May 4 Ambassador Thompson reported from Moscow that the Russians wondered if Kennedy was still interested in seeing Khrushchev. With the report cam hints that Khrushchev might even be willing to avoid talking about such embarrassing—to the U.S.—things as Cuba. Kennedy remained willing: he checked with Republican Richard Nixon, won Nixon's endorsement and the promise that Nixon would publicly approve a Kennedy-Khrushchev meeting even before it was officially announced

(Nixon did so—but with a politically edged suggestion that Kennedy could prove he was strong even though losing his battles). Kennedy also cleared the Vienna meeting with Britain's Harold Macmillan and Franc's De Gaulle. Last week, just before President Kennedy flew off to Canada for a state visit, Soviet Ambassador to the U.S. Mikhail. ('Smiling Mike") Menshikov appeared at the White House with a letter reaffirming Khrushchev's interest in a meeting. Kennedy gave his consent.

State of Disarray. In the past, U.S. Presidents, ranging from Franklin Roosevelt through Harry Truman to Dwight Eisenhower, have never fared too well in face-to-face meetings with Soviet dictators—even when the U.S. was dealing from strength. There was no doubt that Jack Kennedy, his New Frontier foreign policies currently in a state of some disarray, was taking a chance. But Kennedy felt confident that he could look Khrushchev squarely in the eye and effectively warn him that despite recent reverses, neither the President nor the U.S. could safely be pushed around. There were some who argued the necessity of the exercise: the Communists are pretty cock-a-hoop these days, sure that they can toy with the nuclear talks, conquer Laos, wreck the U.N., and maybe start something in Berlin.

There was another consideration beyond Kennedy's making a strong personal impression on Khrushchev. In his inaugural speech, John Kennedy had demanded national sacrifice to meet the challenges of the cold war. "Ask not what your country can do for you," he cried. "Ask what you can do for your country." Since then, President Kennedy has talked often and eloquently of sacrifice—without telling Americans just what they are supposed to do. Presumably, through his personal confrontation with Russia's Nikita Khrushchev, the President can complete his assessment of just how acute he thinks Communism's current threat to be, and what form it will take. Then President Kennedy may be able to come home with specific measures of the sacrifices that the U.S. must make. It so, Vienna will have been of historic value.

But Kennedy's one presidential meeting with Nikita Khrushchev, the Soviet premier, suggests that there are legitimate reasons to fear negotiating with one's adversaries. Although Kennedy was keenly aware of some of the risks of such meetings—his Harvard thesis was titled "Appeasement at Munich"—he embarked on a summit meeting with Khrushchev in Vienna in June 1961, a move that would be recorded as one of the more self-destructive American actions of the cold war, and one that contributed to the most dangerous crisis of the nuclear age.

Senior American statesmen like George Kennan advised Kennedy not to rush into a high-level meeting, arguing that Khrushchev had engaged in anti-American propaganda and that the issues at hand could as well be addressed by lower-level diplomats. Kennedy's own secretary of state, Dean Rusk, had argued much the same in a Foreign Affairs article the previous year: "Is it wise to gamble so heavily? Are not these two men who should be kept apart until others have found a sure meeting ground of accommodation between them?

But Kennedy went ahead, and for two days he was pummeled by the Soviet leader. Despite his eloquence, Kennedy was not match as a sparring partner, and offered only token resistance as Khrushchev lectured him on the hypocrisy of American foreign policy, cautioned America against supporting "old, moribund, reactionary regimes" and asserted that the United States, which had valiantly risen against the British, now stood "against other peoples following its suit." Khrushchev used the opportunity of a face-to-face meeting to warn Kennedy that his country could not be intimidated and that it was "very unwise" for the United States to surround the Soviet Union with military bases.

Kennedy's aides convinced the press at the time that behind closed doors the president was performing well, but American diplomats in attendance, including the ambassador to the Soviet Union, later said they were shocked that Kennedy had taken so much abuse. Paul Nitze, the assistant secretary of defense, said the meeting was "just a disaster." Khrushchev's aide, after the first day, said the American president seemed "very inexperienced, even immature." Khrushchev agreed, noting that the youthful Kennedy was "too intelligent and too weak." The Soviet leader left Vienna elated—and a very low opinion of the leader of the free world.

Kennedy's assessment of his own performance was not less severe. Only a few minutes after parting with Khrushchev, Kennedy, a World War II veteran, told James Reston of the New York Times that the summit meeting had been the "roughest thing in my life." Kennedy went on: "He just beat the hell of of me. I've got a terrible problem if he thinks I'm inexperienced and have not guts. Until we remove those ideas we won't get anywhere with him."

ABOUT THE AUTHOR

MARK BRUCE, DO, FACEP

Mark Bruce was born and raised in the Midwest with a brief three-year early childhood hiatus to Arizona; The Bruce family returned to Arizona and has lived there since 1966. Mark's father was the pastor of churches in Missouri and Arizona. The youngest of three boys, Mark grew up with a love for dogs.

Mark, an emergency medicine physician, spent the early part of his career in the US Navy, and for the last 35 plus years has practiced in Wisconsin. He has been married for 42 years to Moira E. O'Brien-Bruce, DO (family practice/ urgent care), and they have five married adult children; they have three grandsons, and four granddaughters, all of whom are beautiful and geniuses. Mark and Moira's interests include travel and international medical ministry, in Central America, Asia, and Africa. Mark has led many teams into the Asian disaster zones for medical relief work.

In addition to his duties as a staff physician, he serves as the Lead Ambassador to Belize and the Ambassador to Canada for the American College of Emergency Physicians. Mark and Moira are also tutors for the Milwaukee Public Schools. Mark is a member and Elder of New Testament Church in Milwaukee, and a member of the Elmbrook Rotary Club.

JACKIE,
A
BOY,
AND A
DOG
A Warm Cold War Story

MARK D. BRUCE